Look What I Found!

Look

What I Found!

Marshal T. Case
PHOTOGRAPHS BY THE AUTHOR

DRAWINGS BY MARY LEE HERBSTER

The Chatham Press, Inc. • Riverside, Connecticut
DISTRIBUTED BY THE VIKING PRESS, INC.

To childrens' love for nature . . .
Our hope for the future

ACKNOWLEDGMENTS

I am indebted to many persons for their advice and encouragement in my pursuit of a career in Conservation Education. Among these individuals are my friends and associates in Nature Centers, Science Museums and Audubon Societies; my Cornell University professors, Dr. Howard Evans, Dr. David Pimentel, Dr. Verne Rockcastle and Dr. Lowell Uhler, with special thanks to my good friend and favorite professor, Dr. Richard B. Fischer; my parents, Helen and Melville Case, and Edgar and Evelyn Whiting; and, with deepest gratitude, my wife, Nancy.

Thanks are also due Christopher Harris for his design and layout of this book; John Hinshaw for his editorial suggestions and encouragement; Christine O'Shea for assembling the manuscript; and Julia Hinshaw, who first said "Look What I Found!"

—MARSHAL T. CASE
February 21, 1971

Copyright © 1971 by Marshal T. Case

All rights reserved. No part of this book may be reproduced in any form or by any means, mechanical or electronic, except for passages quoted for purposes of review, without permission of its publishers, The Chatham Press, Inc., Riverside, Conn. 06878.

Library of Congress Catalog Card No.: 79-148578
Trade edition: SBN 85699-023-X
Library edition: SBN 85699-024-8

Printed in the United States of America by Eastern Press, Inc.

Contents

1. **THE YOUNG CONSERVATIONIST** 7
2. **A HABITAT AT HOME** 11
   Terrariums, Aquariums, Cages, Collecting Equipment.
3. **INSECTS** 17
   Dragonflies and Damselflies, Caddisfly Larvae, Back Swimmers, Caterpillars, Praying Mantids, Ants, Pet Food Insects.
4. **MARINE AQUARIA** 31
   Fish, Crabs, Barnacles, Sea Anemones, Snails, Starfish.
5. **AMPHIBIANS** 39
   Frogs, Toads, Salamanders.
6. **REPTILES** 47
   Turtles, Snakes, Lizards.
7. **MAMMALS** 57
   Wild Mice, Squirrels, Rabbits, Raccoons, Skunks.
8. **WILD BIRDS** 69
   Feeders, Bird Houses, Caring for Injured and Orphan Birds.
9. **PET SHOP ANIMALS** 79
   Tropical Fish, Flying Squirrels, Guinea Pigs and Hamsters, Gerbils.

   ADDITIONAL READING 91

   INDEX 93

CHAPTER 1

The Young Conservationist

"CONSERVATION" IS A VERY BROAD, MUCH TALKED-ABOUT SUBJECT today. It involves the "conserving" or preservation of all our natural resources, including air, land, water, and plant and animal life. Many people think of conservation as something to be left to the experts: "What can I do that will make any difference?" The answer is that *everyone* must do his part if progress is to be made, and the heaviest burden lies with the younger generation.

This book is concerned primarily with one aspect of conservation; the wild animals of our woods, fields and waters who may not survive unless we make an all-out effort to protect them, as well as the environment we share with them. Many of these animals find their way into our homes and schools each year. Some have fallen or strayed from their nests or burrows; others are orphans whose mothers have been killed by automobiles, hunters or chemical poisoning; still more are simply found and carried home or to classrooms by children.

Most of us have a natural curiosity about animals, and a sincere desire to love and care for them. The experience of raising, handling and observing small wild creatures can be very rewarding. By taking in an orphan, caring for it until it can fend for itself, then releasing it back to the wild, you have "conserved" one small, but important, part of nature. Many animals have fascinating life cycles and habits which can be observed best over a period of time in captivity. By handling, feeding and watching them, you become an amateur zoologist, and at the same time will gain a better understanding of the reasons for conservation. Your success will depend upon your knowledge of the animal's needs, proper feeding and cleanliness, and your desire to return a healthy creature to its native habitat.

Most of the public's conservation education has been accomplished through nature centers, conservation organizations and science museums. These groups include people who are trained in the needs and care of the animals discussed in this book as well as many others which you may encounter.

If you are interested in purchasing a wild animal from a pet shop or considering a field trip to collect some, it is wise to check first with one of these conservation groups, especially if the animal you have in mind for a pet is one of the "exotic" species. The naturalists at these centers will be glad to discuss the animal's needs with you; his advice will make the care of the animal easier for you and help assure it of a long and comfortable life.

Many nature centers and science museums offer special "Junior Staff" programs which allow you to help care for the animals on display and assist in other nature activities. Joining one of these programs is probably the best way to become acquainted with the ways of wild animals and the proper methods to use in caring for them.

The animals which you will learn about in this book are those most likely to be found in your yard, park or wild areas and which can safely be brought home for observation and as study projects. With very few exceptions, these creatures should be kept only a short while, then released where you found them, and thus they are called *short-term* pets. In addition, the last chapter will tell you about some other animals you can buy at pet shops — and some you shouldn't buy!

As often as possible, go on walks in the country, through the mountains or along the seashore. As you observe nature, think of how the world would be without its woodlands, fields, forests and deserts; and without the millions of different kinds of insects, amphibians, reptiles, mammals and birds that inhabit them. Think, too, of the ponds and streams, lakes and oceans, without their fish and other forms of living creatures.

When you do this, you will begin to understand the meaning of conservation, and why conservationists devote their lives to preserving what natural resources we have left, not only for the enjoyment, but for the continued existence of future generations. You can contribute greatly to their work by doing your best to observe basic rules of conservation, and by making it your business to get your friends to observe these rules. If everybody does a little bit, considerable progress will be achieved. Here are a few ways in which you can start — how many other rules can you add to the list?

1. Know what plants and animals are protected by law in your state. Ask your local fish and game warden, nature center or humane society about these laws, and never violate them.
2. Do not touch the nests of birds or burrows of animals. The parents may abandon the young if their homes are disturbed by people.
3. If you roll logs over or look under rocks, place them back as you found them. Many animals depend on these for shelter. If their homes are exposed to open air and sunlight, they will be destroyed.
4. Dead trees are homes for many animals — leave them standing.
5. Do not pick wildflowers or snap limbs from bushes or trees — leave them for other people to enjoy.
6. Never collect more wild animals than you can care for at home. When you are ready to release them, take them back to the place where you found them.
7. Carry an extra collecting bag with you and pick up litter. Leave the open areas cleaner than you found them.

CHAPTER 2

A Habitat at Home

EVERY ANIMAL HAS ITS OWN SPECIAL KIND OF PLACE TO LIVE; A PLACE which we call its "habitat." Your own house and neighborhood, or your apartment building and nearby streets, are your habitat. In the same way, wild animals have many different habitats. Some, such as birds and squirrels, live in trees. Others like rabbits, foxes, chipmunks and many more, live on the ground in burrows, piles of rocks or dead tree stumps. Still more creatures, such as frogs, salamanders and fish, make their homes on the edges of ponds or streams or under the water. How many other animals can you think of that might be found in these different habitats?

When people go camping in the woods, they are visiting a wild habitat, but they usually bring with them a part of their own home — a tent, sleeping bags, cooking pots and canned food. In the same way, when you bring a wild animal from its home into yours, you must give it a place to live that contains the most important things it has left behind.

There are three basic kinds of houses you can make for wild animals; the one you choose should be most like your animal's own habitat. These are (1) "terrariums" which are containers that have mostly dirt or rocks, (2) "aquariums" which are containers filled with water, and (3) wire cages, or boxes with wire tops. Here are several suggestions for building these houses; you can probably think up others.

A wide-mouth jar makes an inexpensive aquarium for a bullfrog tadpole.

Terrariums

A terrarium is a container with dirt, sand or gravel, some rocks and often a few plants. It is a small piece of a ground habitat which might range from very dry (if you live in Arizona) to quite wet (if your animal comes from the edge of a pond).

Terrariums can be set up in many different sizes and shapes, depending upon what kind of animal you wish to have make its home there. A glass or plastic fish tank, which you can buy for as little as three dollars and can use later as an aquarium, makes an excellent terrarium. If you cannot afford to buy a tank, you can use a wide-mouth glass container such as a gallon mayonnaise or candy jar. A smaller jar will do, but be certain it is large enough to give your animal plenty of room to move about. Punch holes in the lid from the *inside* to avoid sharp edges sticking down in the jar. You can also make a top from a round piece of screen wire or plastic mesh bent over the mouth of the jar and held in place with a rubber band. Screen wire, however, should not be used for frogs, snakes and other animals which might injure their skin or scales by rubbing against it.

A terrarium such as the one shown below can also be constructed

A terrarium made from window glass and plastic tape.

with window-pane glass and plastic tape. To make this type of terrarium, obtain six pieces of 9x12-inch window glass from your local hardware store.

First, place strips of strong plastic tape on the four edges of the bottom piece. Next, add the four side pieces, and run tape up each outside edge to secure them. Now add the top, which is hinged at the back by another strip of tape. Finally, be sure to cover all exposed edges of glass with tape so you will not cut yourself on sharp glass. One last piece of tape is added to the top as a handle for opening. Set the terrarium in a shallow aluminum baking pan to avoid damaging the table top or window sill on which you keep it. A small wooden wedge under the top will allow air to circulate inside and prevent the glass from collecting condensation.

An inexpensive aquarium serves as a terrarium for a pickerel frog.

Aquariums

An aquarium is very much like a terrarium, except that it must be able to hold water. The word "aquarium" includes the Latin word "aqua" meaning water, while "terrarium" includes "terra" meaning land or earth.

The simplest aquarium is the same large jar you might have used for your terrarium. Inexpensive plastic aquariums can be purchased for around three dollars and up; others, made of glass with metal frames can range from five or six dollars to several hundred dollars. Large glass jars or all-plastic containers make the best inexpensive salt-water aquariums because they do not have steel frames which can corrode. More expensive salt-water aquariums have aluminum frames. Aquarium equipment can include air pumps, heaters, water thermometers and hood lights, but these need not be purchased until you decide upon the kind of aquatic life you want to keep.

Junior Naturalists help collect and mark turtles for a supervised population study carried out by a Nature Center.

Cages

A simple, but temporary cage, can be made from a large cardboard or wooden box with no top. Cut a piece of wire mesh — anything from screen wire to chicken wire will do — that is three or four inches wider all around than the opening to your box. Place it on top of the box, bend over the edges and lay a piece of wood across the top to keep it down. This will hold most animals if you want to keep them only a short while, or until you can build a more permanent cage.

The best cage for squirrels, rabbits, land turtles and many other animals is one made of wire and wood. The top and often the back should be of plywood; the bottom and remaining sides of wire mesh. The size you make the cage and strength of the wire mesh used depends upon how big an animal you plan to keep. A gerbil, for example, does not need nearly as large or strong a cage as a raccoon.

Collecting Equipment

The best container for collecting anything ranging in size from insects to small frogs or salamanders is a plastic refrigerator box or a large plastic ice cream container with holes punched in the top. *Do not* carry glass jars with you on a hike because they can easily break if you fall or drop them. An old pillow case or laundry bag tied at the top is very useful for holding larger frogs and snakes. A minnow net or butterfly net (depending upon what you expect to find) will make catching much easier. Kitchen strainers with short handles and small wire mesh also make good, inexpensive collecting equipment, particularly for ponds and seashore areas.

One very important collecting rule is: *when you have live creatures in any container, never leave it in the sun!* The air or water inside will soon heat up, and the animal will suffer or die.

We have talked about three kinds of houses for wild animals — terrariums, aquariums and cages — and the basic things you need to bring animals home. Each kind of house has its special use, depending upon the kind of wild animal you want to catch and keep in your home or school. In the chapters that follow, you will learn about the animals themselves; what they eat, where and how they live, and most important, how to care for them.

CHAPTER 3

Insects

INSECTS CAN PROVIDE A GREAT DEAL OF ENJOYMENT AND INTEREST. There are more different types of insects in the world than all the other kinds of animals put together. Scientists have found over nine hundred thousand varieties, and they believe that there are many more yet to be discovered! Insects live almost everywhere on the earth's surface, from frozen mountain peaks and arctic tundra to the driest deserts and wettest jungles. For this reason insects can be found and studied in the city, suburbs and country — no matter where you live!

In this book we will tell you about a few insects which you can find in the woods, streams, parks or in your own yard, and which make good short-term pets. Several books listed under Additional Reading will tell you much more about insects if you decide to study them in more detail.

Insects belong to a group of animals known as *Invertebrates,* which means "having no backbone." This separates them from the vertebrate, or backboned, animals that include mammals, birds, reptiles, amphibians and fish. All true insects have six legs and a body that is divided into three sections. The first section, called the *head,* contains the insect's brain, antennae (feelers), eyes and mouth. The middle part is the *thorax*. This is the "motor room" which houses the muscles used for flying, walking and swimming. The insect's legs and wings are always attached to this section. The final part is the *abdomen,* which contains the stomach and excretory (waste removing) organs, the reproductive organs and, in some insects such as bees and wasps, the stinger.

Almost all types of insects lay eggs, although a few bear their young

A dragonfly at rest on goldenrod.

alive. After hatching, the young, which are wingless and often look nothing like their parents, go through one or more phases in their cycle of development into adult forms. The first phase after the egg hatches is called the "larva" or "nymph" stage — the two words mean almost the same thing. Many nymphs change directly into the adult stage, usually passing through a series of skin-shedding processes. Others, such as caterpillars (which are butterfly or moth nymphs) enter a second phase called the "pupa" stage. During this period the animal encloses itself in a protective cocoon or sealed shelter where it remains inactive for a period of time. Finally, the nymph sheds its last skin, or the pupa opens, and the adult insect emerges. It then flies off, deposits its eggs, and the cycle starts all over again.

Many people think all small creatures that crawl are insects. There is another group of invertebrates, however, that are called *Arachnids*. These are related to insects, but they have only two main body parts, four pairs of legs, and never have wings or antennae. The most common arachnids you find are spiders, ticks, mites, scorpions and harvestmen (daddy longlegs). Since some of these are poisonous to one degree or another,

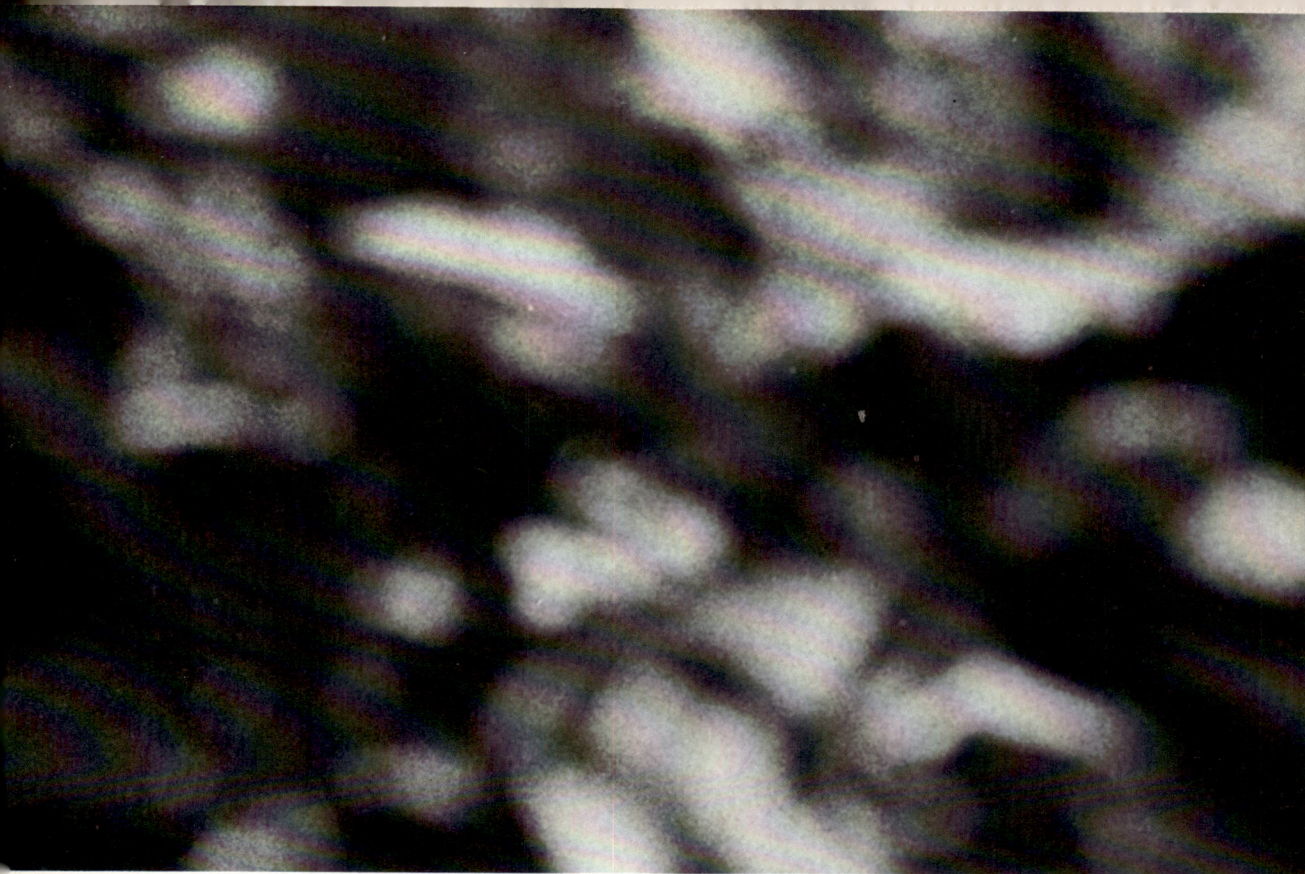

they are not recommended as pets unless you are very familiar with their characteristics and want to make a special study project on them.

A few common insects are easy to catch, or raise, and keep in your home "insectarium" — a terrarium or aquarium set up for insects. All of them have interesting life cycles and habits which can be studied in the field and then observed over a longer period of time in your insectarium.

Dragonflies and Damselflies

Sit quietly on the bank of a pond, lake or stream and watch the air, water and plants around you. At first there seems to be little moving, but if you take a closer look, you will see many interesting insects crawling, swimming and flying about. One of the most fascinating of these is the ferocious-looking dragonfly. Do not be frightened by dragonflies, for although the large ones have a fierce appearance, they cannot sting, bite or scratch you. They are helpful to man because they catch and eat many thousands of mosquitoes, gnats and other small insects that do bite you!

If you watch carefully and long enough, you may even observe a dragonfly catch its food. It does this by flying after smaller insects, holding its legs together like a basket. When it has captured its prey, the dragonfly grasps it with its legs and eats it in flight.

Some adult dragonflies can fly as fast as fifty miles an hour, and are constantly darting about above the surface of the water or taking off straight up from vegetation like a helicopter. Because they are useful creatures in the wild and need a lot of room to fly about, they should not be brought into your home. Instead, look for the dragonfly nymphs and collect some in a container. These nymphs hatch from eggs that are deposited on the leaves and stems of water plants by the adult dragonfly. You can find the nymphs by looking on the undersides of rocks in shallow water or on partially submerged branches or dead logs.

The nymph is a stoutly built animal with a big head and mouth, no wings and, like the parent, a rather ferocious appearance. However, it is completely harmless and you need not hesitate to pick it up. If you look closely at a nymph's mouth, you will see its amazing lower jaw which darts quickly in and out to catch food.

When you bring your nymphs home, take enough pond water to fill about two inches of your aquarium. Lay two or three flat stones in the water, and stand some twigs partly in and partly out of the water so the nymphs can find shelter. If you keep tadpoles in the aquarium, the nymphs will eat them, so don't try to raise dragonflies and frogs together! Nymphs can be fed small earthworms, aquatic insects and even bits of raw liver.

For an interesting experiment, place a nymph in a shallow white dish with just enough water to cover its body, and put a drop of ink or food coloring near its abdomen. You will notice a swirling motion in the

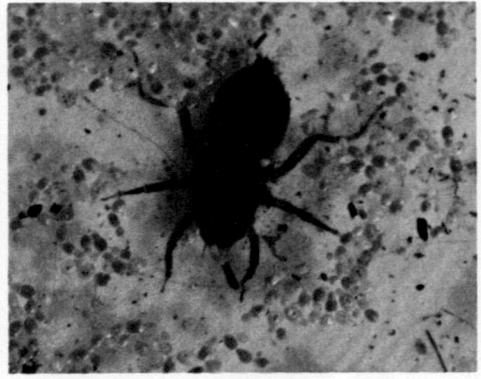 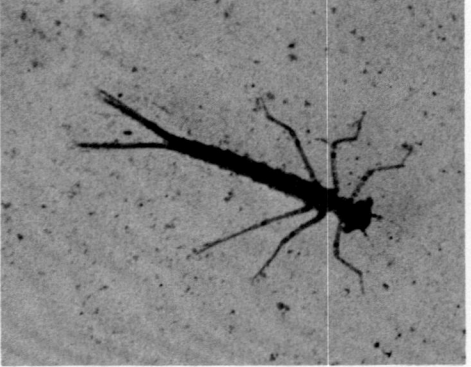

Dragonfly nymph (left) has a stout body while the damselfly nymph (right) is elongated and has plumed gills. Pond animals such as these are easily observed in white plastic pails.

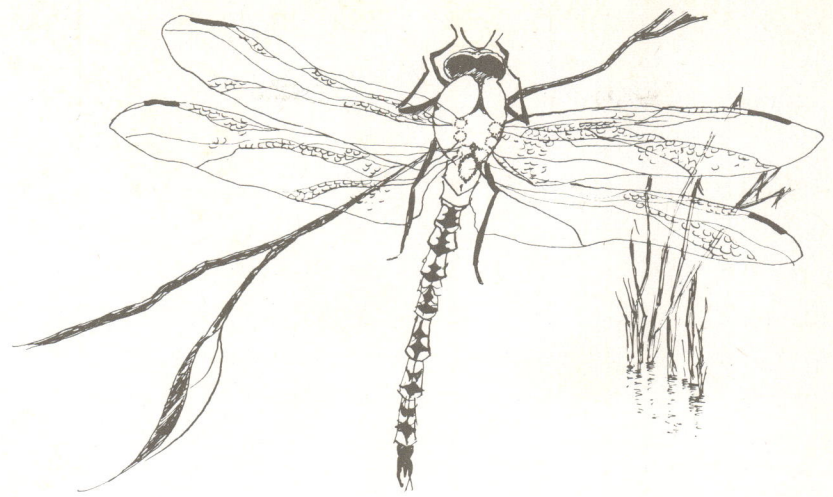

colored water caused by the animal's breathing. It is taking water in through its gills and removing the oxygen, then exhaling a jet of water from its abdomen. When excited, it can eject a stream powerful enough to make it jump forward.

When the nymph is ready to change into adult form, it will crawl out of the water, its skin will split down the middle and an adult dragonfly will emerge. The wet wings of the adult will be crumpled together at first, but they soon dry and the dragonfly is ready to fly. Now is the time to release it. Take it outside, turn it loose and it will find its way to the nearest pond.

A close relative of the dragonfly is the damselfly. It is smaller, has a thinner body and holds its wings over its back like a tent when at rest. It has a fluttering flight, as opposed to the strong movements of the dragonfly. This nymph hatches out of eggs in the water just as the dragonfly nymph does and the life cycle is the same. It is found in the same places as the dragonfly nymph and can be recognized by the external plumed, flat gills on the end of the abdomen.

Caddisfly Larvae

Another insect that is fun to study is the caddisfly. As adults, caddisflies are mothlike in appearance and have a very short life span. The larvae resemble worms with legs on one end of their bodies, and form two different types of cases. One, which is found under stones in stream beds, looks

Caddisfly larvae housings made from pond vegetation are attached to submerged bark.

like a small tube made of cemented pebbles or sand grains. They are often attached to stones, but with a little pull you can free them. Be careful, however, not to crush the cases by squeezing them too hard. Place a case in a container of pond water and wait a few minutes. Soon you will see a small head and some legs appear. The larvae move along the bottom of the pond on these legs and carry their cases on their backs for protection. You may find some cases that are sealed up. These are ready to change into adult forms and have closed themselves inside to go through the pupal stage. When ready, they will cut their way out, swim to the surface and emerge as adult caddisflies. The adults are rarely seen, for they live only a few days.

The other common caddisfly larva case is found in the bottom vegetation of ponds. Squat on the edge of a pond and watch the bottom for signs of movement in the mud and plants. At first it may appear that the vegetation itself is moving or something is pushing the plants aside as it crawls among them. On closer observation, you will see a tube of crossed pieces of vegetation, resembling the construction of a log cabin. This kind of caddisfly larva has constructed its protective house out of bits of aquatic plants.

Take one or two of these interesting creatures home and try an experiment. First, fill a glass jar aquarium with pond water. Then carefully remove the cases from the larvae's backs, place the animals in the aquarium and drop a handful of glass beads or bits of styrofoam in with them. Leave the aquarium overnight and the next morning you may find that the caddisfly larvae have made new houses from the beads or styrofoam. What shape are the new houses? Will all of the larvae you collect build the same shape houses from materials that they have never used? Try some.

Back Swimmers

While you are watching the edge of a pond, you may see a swimming insect that appears to hang downward in the water when it rests. This is the back swimmer. It has a groove surrounded by hairs on the underside of its body that forms a chamber into which air is forced by the hind legs. When it dives, the back swimmer carries this bubble of air with it, allowing it to breathe below the surface for as long as several hours. If you collect one, be careful. It has a stinger in its beak with which it paralyzes and captures small aquatic animals for food, and it can give you a slightly painful, though harmless, sting. If you take one home, put it in a small aquarium similar to that described for the dragonfly nymph. Feed it mosquito wrigglers, and observe how it swims, dives and captures food.

Caterpillars

Most of us have seen caterpillars at one time or another; they are the larvae of butterflies or moths, and are fascinating short-term pets to observe as they spin their cocoons, go through the pupal stage and finally emerge to spread their wings and fly off. A good time of year to collect caterpillars is mid or late summer, just before many of them spin their cocoons. They live in every part of the woods, fields, backyards, even on sand dunes near beaches — in fact, almost everywhere that there are growing plants — and are sometimes found in large swarms.

The monarch butterfly begins life as a caterpillar, then spins a cocoon in which it rests through the pupal stage until emerging as an adult butterfly.

23

When you find a caterpillar, put it in a collecting jar along with a supply of the leaves from the tree or plant on which you found it. These leaves are important because the caterpillar is a fussy eater — different varieties of caterpillars will eat only certain kinds of leaves. The monarch butterfly caterpillar, for example, feeds only on leaves of the milkweed plant.

At home, set up a glass jar terrarium with a screen top. Put your caterpillar and leaves inside, and sprinkle the terrarium lightly with water every two or three days to keep it moist.

The caterpillar will stop feeding shortly before it is ready to spin its cocoon. Just behind the mouth of the caterpillar is a large structure that includes an organ called a "spinneret", which creates the material that forms the cocoon. Most cocoons are created in a few minute's activity and thus you probably will not see the spinning process unless you watch for the moment when the caterpillar begins to wriggle about and start its weaving. Once the caterpillar is enclosed in the cocoon, its body changes from the larval to the pupal phase, during which time it remains inactive. This period of change can take several weeks or months depending on the type of moth or butterfly until, finally, the adult emerges. You can distinguish an adult moth from an adult butterfly by the hairy and stout appearance of the moth's body, as opposed to the slimmer, more silken look of the butterfly. Like dragonflies, butterflies and moths need room to fly about, and should always be released outside as soon as they emerge from their cocoons.

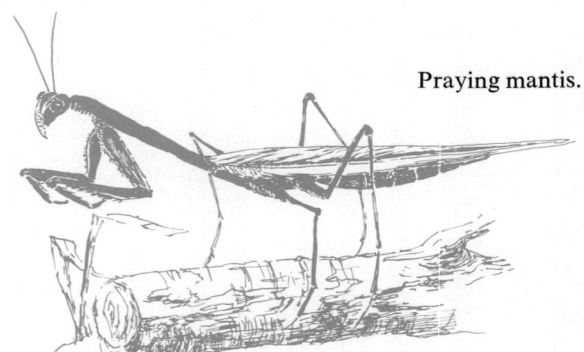

Praying mantis.

Praying Mantids

The praying mantis is another strange-looking insect that is entirely harmless to people and makes one of the best short-term pets. Its name, *praying* mantis, is descriptive of the way in which it sits motionless among the weeds or shrubs, its long legs folded reverently, waiting for some moving object to come within reach. Then one might say it becomes a *preying* mantis, as its forelegs dart out and clamp shut on its unfortunate victim.

When you find a praying mantis, catch it quickly or it will fly away. Bring it home and place it in a screen-covered terrarium with soil and some green weeds on the bottom and small twigs or sticks that are propped upright against the sides so the mantis can crawl on them. Your mantis will eat many different kinds of insects, including grasshoppers, flies and beetles, but it will not eat ants. Never put two mantids in the same terrarium, as the larger one will probably eat the smaller.

Because praying mantids sit almost upright on stems or twigs and seem to look at you with large eyes, they are familiar subjects for insect photographers. If you have a camera that can take close-up photos, try capturing your mantis on film.

In the fall, you may find what looks like a large brown or brownish-yellow cocoon stuck to a weed, shrub or the side of a building. This is the egg case of a praying mantis. Take it home and place it in a terrarium. Put the terrarium in a cool corner of your house where you can leave it until spring. During the winter months keep the terrarium moist with a few sprinkles of water each week. By April, if you are lucky, you will see the egg case begin to hatch. As many as two hundred baby mantids will emerge. Soft at first, their shells soon harden and they are ready to begin life. Release them in your yard and watch for them during the summer.

A close relative of the praying mantis is the walking stick. This curious insect looks exactly like its name — a stick with legs. It is much harder to find than the mantis, partly because it is not as common and partly because it has better camouflage. If you do find one, however, put it in the same kind of terrarium as described for a praying mantis. Walking sticks feed on leaves of trees, especially oak and cherry, instead of other insects.

Ants

Ants are familiar to everyone. No matter where you live, these insects can be found close by — in fields, woods, meadows, along sidewalks of city streets and even in your own house or apartment building. There are around ten thousand different kinds of ants living on all the continents of the earth. As you observe and read about ants, you will discover many kinds with special ways of life or activities. To name a few of the most interesting ones, there are carpenter ants, harvester ants, honey ants, army ants and leaf-cutting ants.

Ants are born from eggs and go through the larval and pupal stages before becoming adults. Females dominate the colonies, as the males are only needed for the marriage flights. The queen is the largest ant of the colony, and she is surrounded by infertile females which do the work of finding food, tending the eggs, larvae and pupae, defending the ant colony, digging tunnels, building nests and caring for the queen. Ants are social insects; they depend on each other, work together and share everything.

Have fun observing ants outdoors. Look for them in open fields (where they make mounds of fine soil excavated from their underground houses), in rock crevices, under flat rocks and old lumber, crawling on trees or in the cracks of sidewalks. You may discover two different kinds fighting in one area — different colonies battle each other! Have you ever noticed an ant carrying a caterpillar or a dead bee? An ant can lift up to fifty times its own weight. Ants are also capable of learning their way through mazes or when to expect food; young ants soon learn to recognize the odor of their own colony. Ants are also one of the cleanest of the insects. Watch them stroke their antennae with special hair combs on their legs and lick each other with their tongues to keep clean.

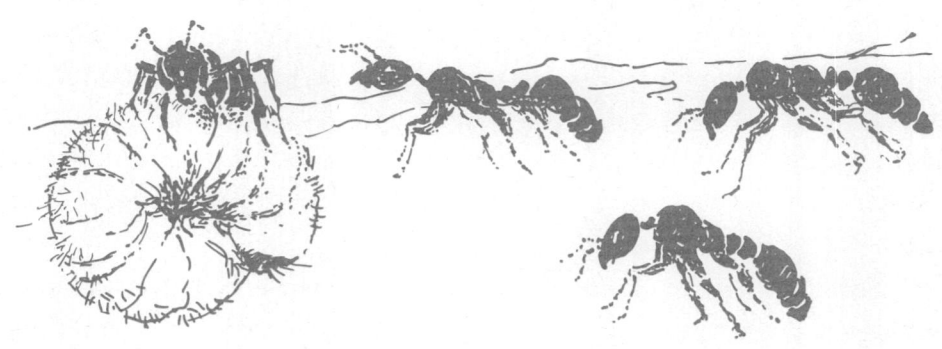

An ant house is easy to build.

You can build your own ant observation house or buy one at a pet store. To make your own, get two panes of glass about twelve inches square, and fit them into two upright grooved pieces of wood the same size, with a third piece of wood on the bottom to act as a stand. A top can be fitted into the slot of the glass with the sides extending over the glass, or hinged to one side with a clasp on the other side. Two holes bored in the top and covered tightly with fine screening serve for watering and ventilation. You can also tie small pieces of sponge, one soaked with water and another covered with honey or other food, to a string and drop them down within reach of the ants.

When your ant house is ready, take a closed container, gardening gloves and a trowel to a place where you have observed an ant colony mound. Quickly shovel earth and ants into your container, and wear gloves as ants can bite when disturbed. Try to locate and capture the one ant that appears larger than the others, the queen, so your colony can continue to breed in captivity.

Take them home and pour the earth and ants into your ant house, filling it about two-thirds full. If you are going to use sponges on strings for feeding, now is the time to suspend these from the screening. Honey, boiled eggs and bread are also good food for the ants.

For a school or home study project, make daily observations of your colony and record what you see in a notebook. How long does it take for them to settle in their new quarters? Can you see them making tunnels? Do they lick each other and use their special combs to keep clean? A large magnifying glass will enlarge the ants and make your observations more fun. Try making some pencil sketches of ants and their activities in your notebook.

Pet-Food Insects

Several insects can be raised as food supplies for other wild animals. A black or brown beetle, commonly found in city parks, woods or in and around barns in the country, lay eggs that produce meal worms. If you cannot find these beetles, buy a few meal worms at your local pet store (usually a penny each) and start your own colony. All you need, beside the worms, is a small cardboard box, cookie tin or cigar box, some corn flakes, bran meal or corn meal, and some apple slices. Place your meal worms in the container with the meal and a few slices of apple. After several weeks you will see some of the meal worms turn into white, stout pupae. Later the pupae change into beetles, and the beetles die shortly after laying eggs on the apple slices. When the eggs hatch into meal worms, you have a complete life cycle, and from then on your colony will continue to replenish its numbers. Meal worms are eaten by turtles, snakes, salamanders, lizards, frogs and toads, fish and even by some mammals.

Another easy insect to raise is the fruit fly. Place a piece of banana or apple in an open container outdoors. Soon small flies will land on the fruit, especially during warm days in the spring, summer and fall. Let them swarm about for a few days and lay their eggs on the fruit. Then cover the container with fine mesh screening. In a few days you will see many small maggots or white worms swarming over the fruit — this is

A meal worm "farm" will provide a year-round food supply for many animals.

the larval form of the fruit fly. Next, the pupae will appear on the sides of the container in the form of small brown oval tubes. The final stage takes place when the adult fruit flies emerge from the pupal cases. Now you are ready to start another colony.

CHAPTER 4

Marine Aquaria

THOSE OF YOU WHO ARE FORTUNATE ENOUGH TO LIVE NEAR OR VISIT THE seashore have an abundant new world to explore — the realm of the saltwater animal communities. Within the tidal zones, among rocks and jetties, along beaches and mud or sand flats, and throughout salt marshes, thousands of different creatures live out their varied lives. In this book we can only touch on a few of the most common of these animals; for those who wish more detailed knowledge several excellent books are listed in the Additional Reading section.

Marine aquaria are easy to set up and maintain, especially if you intend to make short-term summer pets of the animals you collect. Once you have an aquarium established, you can change the animal life as often as you go to your various collecting areas, releasing some animals and adding new ones.

The best container for a small marine aquarium is a three- to five-gallon clear plastic fish tank. This can be purchased for only a few dollars at most pet or hardware stores. Temporary marine aquaria can also be made from large-mouth jars, as described in Chapter Two.

On your first trip to the shore, bring home a small pail full of dry sand, a larger container of salt water, several rocks, and a few animal specimens which interest you. Do not include any seaweed, as most species soon decay in an aquarium and foul the water in the process. The

The green crab with eight legs is a variety of walking crabs. Swimming crabs have fin-like appendages in place of their two rear legs.

best container for transporting salt water by car is a small plastic garbage pail with a top that locks on by the handles. This will not spill or slop water, and can carry several smaller pails full of collected material as well as the water.

Place about two inches of sand in the bottom of your tank, then slowly pour in the salt water and add your rocks. An electric air pump should be used to aerate the water gently if you plan to keep the aquarium longer than a few days. Place the aquarium in a spot where it is out of direct sunlight.

When you have filled the tank about three-quarters full, mark the water level on the outside with a crayon or small piece of adhesive tape. As the water evaporates, add more *fresh* water to bring the level back to your mark. Fresh water is added because only the water evaporates — not its salt and mineral content. Thus if you add more salt water, you will increase the salinity (salt content) of your tank and kill the marine life. Siphon or dip out about one-third of the water every two weeks and add new salt water to keep the tank fresh and renew the small food supply.

When your aquarium is ready, collect two or three of each of the creatures you find and want to observe. Be sure not to over-crowd the tank; you can always change animals. Some of the most interesting to watch are described in the sections that follow.

Fish

One of the easiest salt-water animals to keep is the killifish, known to most people as a minnow or chub. You will find them swimming in schools just beyond the tide line or in tidal pools and streams of salt marshes. When you frighten a school, watch how every fish turns almost at the same instant and darts away. Catch a few in a minnow net or trap and bring them home to your aquarium. There are several varieties of these fish, but the most numerous ones, called common killifish, have a bluish-green shine to their bodies. Feed killifish pieces of earthworm, bits of chopped clams, liver or brine shrimp.

Another interesting, but much more difficult fish to find, is the pipefish. They resemble small blades of eelgrass and are often indistinguishable from the grass beds in which they live. Usually you will find them resting or swimming in an upright position, moving about by means of

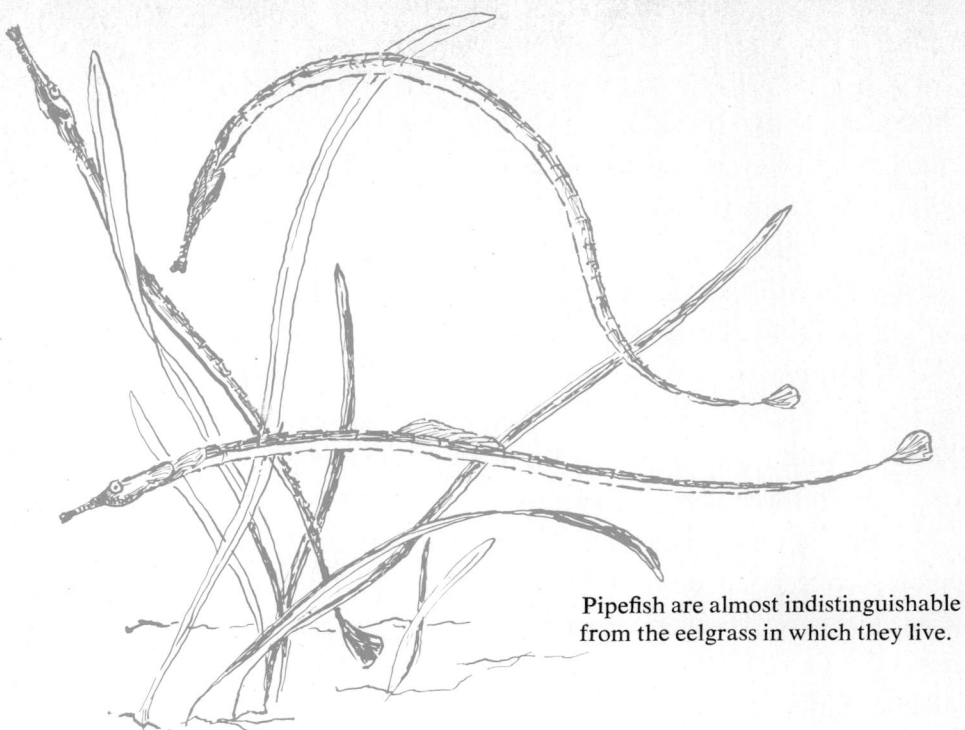

Pipefish are almost indistinguishable from the eelgrass in which they live.

their back (dorsal) fins. If you catch one, notice its long tubular nose, which resembles that of its close relative, the seahorse.

Another unusual feature of pipefish is that the female lays her eggs in a special pouch of the male, who then carries them until the young are born. If you catch a male in late summer, look closely at its pouch. You may see the eggs, or possibly several hundred hatched young with tiny, beady eyes still inside. When the young are ready to be born, the male thrusts them out, a few at a time. They are miniatures of the adult, and only about half an inch long. If you keep pipefish in your aquarium, add new salt water every few days to give them fresh food, or feed them brine shrimp from a pet shop.

Crabs

As you poke around rocks or watch the sandy bottom of a shallow bay near low tide, you will see shells that suddenly sprout legs and pinchers and run about. These are hermit crabs carrying their houses on their backs. This crab has no protective shell of its own, and thus must find safety in a vacant snail shell such as a periwinkle, moon snail or whelk. As the crab grows and becomes too big for the shell it occupies, it looks for a new, larger one and quickly makes a move from the old to the new house. Take two or three home for your aquarium. Include a few empty snail shells of a size slightly larger than those occupied by your crabs, in case one is ready to change its house.

Small hard-shelled crabs of several varieties may also be kept in the aquarium with a minimum of care. If you live near or visit the rocky coast of Maine, you will probably find a rock crab or its slightly larger relative, the Jonah crab. Farther south, along sandy coast lines, are blue crabs, green crabs and Calico crabs. When you pick up a crab, grasp it from the rear with your thumb on the bottom of its shell and your fingers on the top. This way it cannot reach you with its pinchers.

Young horseshoe crabs, two to four inches long, are also very interesting animals to observe for a short time. These creatures are more closely related to spiders than to crabs, and have survived in their present form for some 150 million years. Watch how they feed and move around the aquarium, and compare them with regular crabs — sometimes horseshoe crabs even swim on their backs! See if you can locate their large, compound eyes on the fronts of their shells, and count how many clawed feet they have.

One other kind of crab you will find is the fiddler crab. The male fiddlers can easily be distinguished because they have one very large claw and a second, much smaller claw. These crabs dig burrows in sand banks or mud flats which lie between high and low tide lines. Because they de-

A horseshoe crab.

A cluster of rock barnacles await the tide.

pend upon the rise and fall of the tide to bring them water, food and sunlight, they should not be kept in an aquarium, but are fascinating to watch as they dart to and from the entrances of their homes.

All crabs are scavengers, feeding along the shore line on bits of dead fish, shellfish and algae. Pick some sea lettuce or eelgrass for a temporary food supply. After you have the crabs established in the aquarium, remove the seaweed and feed them bits of chopped clams, fish, liver, hamburger and brine shrimp. When you tire of observing them, return them to the shore area where you found them.

Barnacles

If you scratch your bare feet while making your way across rocks in the tidal zone, it is probably because you stepped on barnacles. These interesting creatures are, believe it or not, related to shrimps. They begin their lives as free swimming larvae, and later attach themselves to rocks, pilings or almost any hard surface that is submerged at high tide. The "glue" with which they stick themselves has amazed scientists for years and they are still unable to reproduce its qualities for human use. Once the larva is firmly attached, it begins to secrete a substance which forms the protective shell around the growing animal.

As you sit on a rock or jetty during an incoming tide, watch the barnacles when the water begins to cover them. The shells, tightly closed to conserve moisture while the tide is out, begin to open as soon as the animals are submerged. A cluster of legs, which somewhat resembles a hand, extends out from the shell, feels for food that is being washed by, then rapidly darts back inside. This motion is repeated over and over as the barnacle feeds on the minute plants and animals known as plankton.

You can observe barnacles in your aquarium if you have an aerator to keep the water in motion. They are simple to collect — just take home a small barnacle-covered rock, bottle or piece of wood. Part of the salt water in the aquarium should be changed frequently to give the barnacles new food supplies.

A sea anemone extends its tentacles in search of food.

Sea Anemones

These animals, which are often mistaken for plants, are shell-less creatures that live in most of the same places as barnacles. They seem to be attached to rocks or pilings, but actually have the ability to move slowly across a hard surface by means of a gliding action in their single foot. Like barnacles, they live by capturing food as it washes over them. When the tide is out they are almost invisible, lying like folded up blobs among the seaweed. As soon as the water covers them, their tentacles extend, searching for prey. Their tentacles have the power to sting small fish, but (except for some warm-water species) they are harmless to man. Thus, you can take home a rock with an attached anemone and watch it in your aquarium. Feed it pieces of liver with a pair of forceps or tweezers and watch how it eats.

Snails

You can find several kinds of marine snails along the shore line, including whelks, moon snails, mud snails and periwinkles. The moon snail is named for its moon-shaped shell. It glides along the sandy bottom on its one large foot and often leaves a trail that looks like someone drew a stick across the sand. When the female is ready to lay its eggs, it pieces sand particles together in the shape of a circle or collar around itself and the eggs are then laid on the inside of this "sand collar." This protects them from fish and other scavengers.

Periwinkles (which have ridged shells) and mud snails (which have smooth shells) are important scavengers along the shore line. At low tide you will see thousands of them gliding across mud and sand flats as they feed on dead plant and animal material. Both are valuable because they help to keep the beaches clean and free of decaying matter. A few periwinkles or mud snails will remove uneaten food and droppings, and keep a proper balance in your aquarium.

Starfish

These animals do not survive long in aquariums because they require special living conditions, but are fun to observe along the shore line and in tidal pools. Starfish have suction-cup feet on the undersides of each of their arms which they use to grasp and open clam and mussel shells for food. If you find a starfish on a cluster of mussels, watch closely as the starfish attaches two arms to one side of a shell and three to the other, with the center of its body directly over the mussel opening. As the tube feet slowly apply an outward pressure, the muscle of the shellfish weakens and finally lets the shell open. The starfish then drops its stomach down into the opening and consumes the meat. If you do take a starfish home, change the aquarium water frequently and keep the animal only a few days.

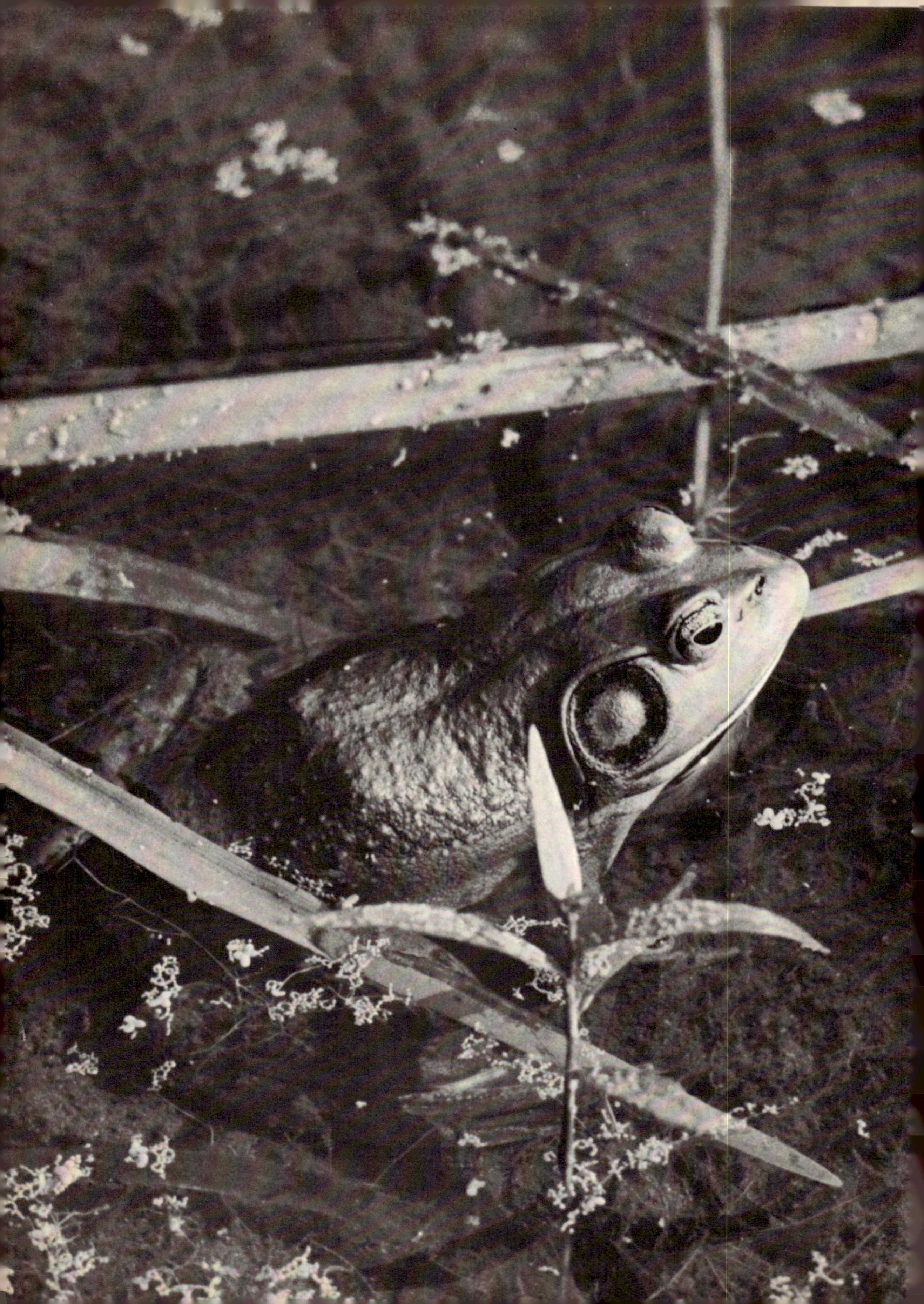

CHAPTER 5

The Amphibians

FROGS, TOADS AND SALAMANDERS ARE GROUPED IN A CLASS KNOWN AS *Amphibians,* a Greek word meaning "double life." They are animals which must stay moist and cool to survive. Their body temperature varies with that of their surroundings, and therefore they are called "cold-blooded" animals. Most amphibians lay eggs in the water or in moist, damp places. The young, called larvae, breathe through gills, while the adults usually have lungs.

Frogs

Frogs and their larvae, called tadpoles or polliwogs, are excellent creatures to keep as pets or for a study project. There are about two thousand different kinds of frogs in the world, ranging in size from twelve inches in length to as small as a penny. Most of them live in or near fresh water, but some have learned to live in trees.

The common frogs you will find have long hind legs with webbed feet for swimming and a moist, smooth skin. They have eyes that somewhat resemble the human eye and which can close from the bottom up. An adult frog breathes air through lungs and through pores in its skin. When swimming under water it closes its nostrils much the same as you might hold your nose!

In the northeastern United States, you are most likely to see the spotted leopard, or grass frog, the green frog and the large bullfrog (shown in the picture opposite). To find them, look along the edge of a pond or stream where they will be sitting next to or directly in the water. Frogs are hard to catch because, as you will discover, they can jump into the water and swim away very quickly. Thus, a long-handled minnow net will be a big help. The best way to hold a frog, once you catch him, is by the upper part of its long hind legs, where they join the body. When held this way, it cannot squirm around and injure itself, nor can it get leverage to leap out of your hands.

Frogs, as well as the other amphibians, should be kept in a terrarium. Put a layer of gravel on the bottom, then some soil, moss, a rock or two and pieces of tree bark. Be sure to include a fairly large, heavy bowl filled with water, and change the water frequently. If you do not want to set up a fancy terrarium, you can simply put in gravel and a couple of rocks, plus the bowl of water. This set-up is easy to clean by simply washing the gravel in a kitchen strainer once a week. Keep a top such as a piece of pegboard, or other board with air holes, on the terrarium, unless you want frogs jumping about your house.

Frogs eat live earthworms, live minnows and live insects such as grasshoppers, crickets and ants. If you keep a frog over the winter, you can raise meal worms and fruit flies such as was described in the chapter on insects, or buy mealworms and night crawlers at a pet shop. Another interesting way to feed your frog is to dangle small bits of lean hamburger or dog food on a thread in front of it. The movement makes the meat seem alive, and the frog will soon learn to grab at it.

In the spring look in quiet water for the frogs' jelly-like egg masses attached to twigs or leaves. If you find some, bring them, twigs and all, home in a collecting container filled with pond water, and transfer this to a larger container of pond water. They should hatch in a few days to two weeks, depending upon how long they were in the pond, and tiny tadpoles emerge. At first they look almost like small fish. Gradually, their bodies grow, and after a few weeks hind legs begin to appear, then the forelegs, until finally the creature becomes an adult frog.

Tadpoles feed on aquatic plants and algae. Therefore, you will have to make a number of trips to the pond where you found the eggs to bring home fresh water plus plant life. Be sure to change at least half of the water every few days. When the frogs reach the adult stage, return most of them to the pond, keeping one or two as pets if you wish to care for them.

If you succeed in raising a few frogs from a mass of eggs, you will have watched one of nature's many fascinating transformations. How does the frog's change from egg to tadpole (larva) to adult compare with the changes that take place in the lives of insects?

Toads

Toads are frequently confused with frogs; both animals have a common name, *Salentia,* which means "the jumping ones". It is not hard, though, to tell them apart. A toad's skin is dry and rough or warty, while frogs are moist and smooth; toads have shorter hind legs than frogs, and hop rather than jump. Generally, they have a fatter, chunkier appearance.

You will find toads in city parks, back yards, fields and woods where they hide under moist leaves or burrow in the ground to stay cool. If you leave an outside light burning or go to a lighted park on summer nights, you can see them hopping about on the grass looking for insects to eat.

A common American garden toad makes a good short-term pet.

Toads live on land most of the time, but in late spring or early summer they make their way to ponds or streams where they lay their eggs in tubular strings wrapped around vegetation just below the surface. Later in the summer you may see many small toads hopping back to the protection of the woods or gardens.

Toads, like frogs, can be kept in terrariums. They need three or four inches of soil on top of a layer of gravel, along with moss, leaves and tree bark, and a shallow bowl of water in which to soak. Be sure this is changed every few days to keep it fresh and clean. Except for minnows, they eat the same live food as frogs, and will take bits of meat dangled from a thread. If you feed them lightning bugs in the summer, you will see the light from the insects glowing through the skin of the toad.

With patience you can train grey tree frogs to wait in line for their meal worms.

The larger animal is a spotted salamander. Can you find the red eft?

Salamanders

These amphibians (which are also called newts) resemble lizards, but again it is easy to tell the two animals apart. Salamanders have smooth skin; lizards are rough or scaly. Lizards also have claws on their toes and ear openings, while salamanders have neither.

Salamanders are harder to find than frogs and toads, mainly because they are more secretive. You will find them hidden under damp beds of decaying leaves, logs or grass piles, or under flat stones in shaded, mossy areas. (Remember to put back overturned logs and rocks — they are shelters for many animals).

Some salamanders, such as the red-spotted newt and the two-lined salamander, will also be found swimming in shallow water near the edge

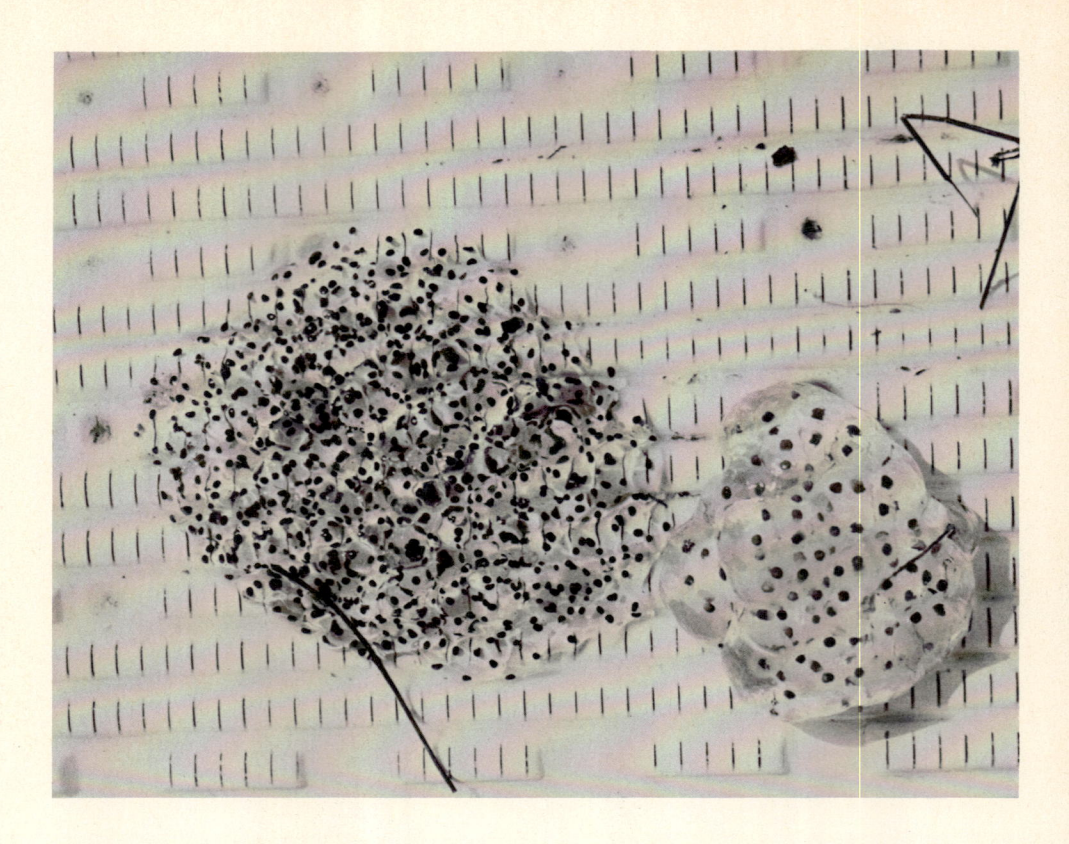

An egg mass of the wood frog (left) has over twice as many tadpoles as that of the spotted salamander (right). Compare these with the drawing of a toad's egg mass.

of a pond or slow-running brook. These species range up to six inches in length. Another salamander, called a mud puppy, can grow as large as two feet long. They have four short legs, strong rudder-like tails, smooth bodies and flat heads. These creatures spend most of their lives in water among aquatic plants at depths up to eight feet.

When you find a salamander you want to bring home, wet your hands before picking it up. This will help keep the animal moist and lessen the danger of injuring it. Have plenty of moist leaves or moss in your collecting container, and *never* leave it in the sun. Salamanders soon die if exposed to heat.

At home, keep the salamander in a terrarium similar to that made for toads. Be sure, however, to sprinkle the terrarium frequently with water to keep it moist inside, and put it in a cool, shaded place. Never leave the terrarium on a window sill, as direct sunlight will harm the salamanders. Salamanders thrive on a diet of live earthworms, slugs and meal worms. If you keep one long enough, and put its food at the same spot in the terrarium, it will learn to come there when hungry.

Like frogs and toads, some salamanders lay their eggs during early spring in jelly-like masses attached to twigs or leaves in shallow water. The spotted salamander's egg mass contains less black dots, which are the new larvae, than the egg mass of the wood frog (see photographs for a comparison). If you collect a salamander egg mass, treat it in the same way as described for frog's eggs. When the young hatch, you will find that they have four limbs and resemble the adult more closely than the tadpole resembles a frog, yet they live like fish until they become adults.

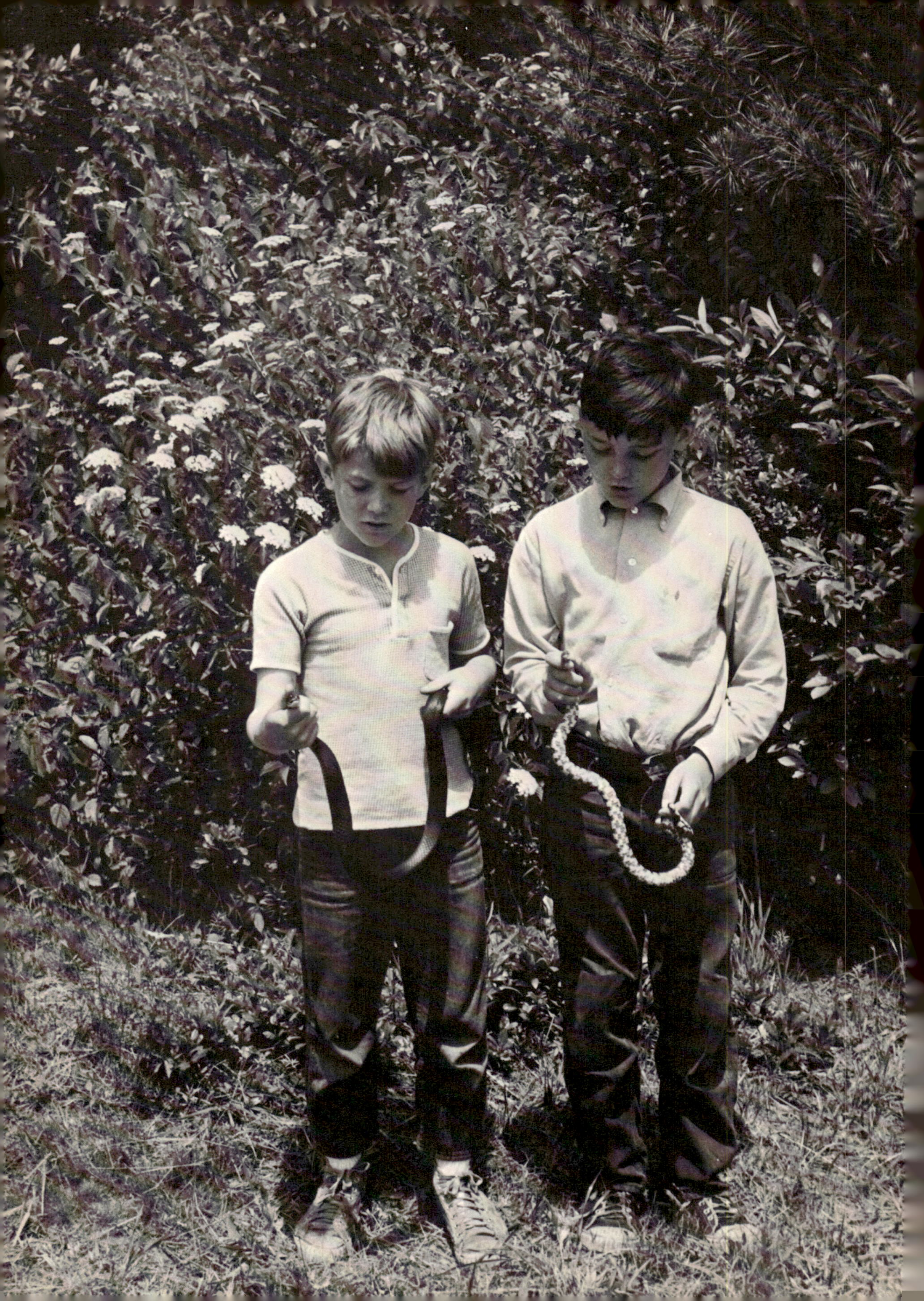

CHAPTER 6

Reptiles

VARIOUS KINDS OF TURTLES, LIZARDS AND SNAKES CAN BE FOUND throughout the United States. These animals, along with alligators and crocodiles, belong to a class called *Reptiles*. They are similar to amphibians in one respect — both are cold-blooded creatures because the temperature of their bodies varies with the temperature of their surrounding environment. Reptiles, however, possess armor or scales for protection and do not need to return to the water to lay their eggs. Thus they are a more advanced form of life, representing a bridge between the amphibian and mammal worlds.

Most reptiles lay eggs, although a few, such as water snakes and garter snakes, give birth to living young. Reptile eggs can be distinguished from bird eggs by their rubbery or spongy shell instead of a brittle one. Inside the shell are membranes that retain moisture and prevent the growing animal from drying out and dying. The eggs are laid by the female reptile in warm sand, decaying wood, or dirt areas which are exposed to the sun, and most are then abandoned. The young hatch in four to twelve weeks and are immediately at the mercy of many predators.

If you find some reptile eggs and want to hatch them, here are two methods you can try. One is to put sand or dirt in a screen-covered window box or other box that gets sun each day, and bury the eggs several inches beneath the surface. If it does not rain frequently, or if your box is inside, sprinkle it with water once a week. Check the box each day

Two young herpetologists hold a northern black racer (left) and an eastern milk snake (right).

Turtles are found in many habitats. To the right is a painted turtle from fresh water ponds and streams. Below is a box turtle which lives in the woods and fields. On the opposite page is a diamondback terrapin which inhabits salt-water marshes from Massachusetts to Texas.

48

toward the end of the first four weeks when the young reptiles should begin to hatch and crawl around on top of the dirt. Another excellent way to hatch snake and turtle eggs is to wrap them in moist paper towels and place them in a covered container in a closet of your house. Change the towels twice a week to keep mold from growing on the eggs. By this method the eggs are kept at a constant temperature and you will have the advantage of looking at them frequently without having to dig them up each time.

Most reptile hatchlings are difficult to feed and house, and should now be released at the place you found the eggs.

Turtles

Of all the reptiles, turtles are the best and most popular to keep as short-term pets. There are many kinds of turtles living on land and in the water. Box turtles, one of the most common land varieties, can be found in fields and thicket areas feeding on wild berries, or, sometimes, lumbering across highways. They are protected by conservation laws in some states, so be sure to check with a nature center or warden before catching one.

If you bring a box turtle home to study, provide it with a large terrarium or cage containing a log, two to three inches of sand or soil, and some leaves. It also needs a large container of water because it will submerge its head while drinking and climb into the water to soak. This can be set up outdoors in the summer, and the turtle kept until mid-September when it should be released. If you keep it into winter in a cold climate, it will try to hibernate and, without sufficient protection, will freeze to death. Even if brought into the house, land turtles will still try to hibernate, stop eating and may starve.

Box turtles, as well as wood and other land turtles, can be fed a wide variety of foods, including earthworms, insects, berries, liver and leafy vegetables, such as fresh spinach and lettuce. They should be fed at least once a day, and any stale or uneaten food should be removed from the cage. Be sure to keep their water fresh.

When you have a turtle for a short-term pet, take some time to study its physical build and habits. The name "box turtle" comes from the use of the protective shell. The lower shell is hinged, and when the box turtle is frightened, it can pull all four legs, the head and tail back inside the shell. The hinge then closes the lower shell against the upper shell, and it is now "boxed in."

What does a box turtle do if it gets turned over on its back? How does it turn itself right side up again? Do turtles have ear openings? And what about teeth? Observe your turtle and see if you can answer these questions.

Of the water turtles, the painted or sun turtles, as they are often called, make good wild pets. They are found along the edges of ponds where you can catch them with your hands (if you are quick), in a net, or on a fish hook baited with bacon.

Painted turtles get their name from the red and yellow patterns on their shells and the yellow lines on their heads. They must be kept in an aquarium which is deep enough for them to swim in but which also has a large, flat rock, partly out of the water, on which they can sun. Place the aquarium in a window where it will receive several hours of sunlight each day. Change the water twice a week, and be sure the clean water is at room temperature before you put it in the tank. A sudden change of water temperature can harm the turtles, especially during winter months. These turtles eat meal worms, earthworms, minnows and insects, or even fresh lettuce and bits of chopped liver.

Another interesting fresh water turtle is the musk turtle. These animals live in the same areas as painted turtles, and can sometimes be taken on a fish hook. Musk turtles, however, forage for food by crawling along the bottom of ponds or streams rather than swimming. They resemble oval-shaped rocks, and have been nicknamed "Stinkin' Jim" or "Stinkpots" because they can give off a strong, foul odor when angry.

If you bring one home, place it in an aquarium with four to five inches of water and some exposed rocks, gravel or dirt. It can be fed almost anything, including scraps from your dinner table, and will thrive indoors throughout the winter.

A WORD OF CAUTION: When you are looking for turtles or other pond creatures, be sure you do not catch snapping turtles! These can be distinguished by their thickset, powerful appearance, large head and long tail. They strike with great speed; large ones are able to take your finger off, and even babies can bite. If you see a snapping turtle, simply leave it alone and it will not bother you.

Snakes

When you are walking through fields or woods, you may come upon a snake sunning itself in the path or slithering off through the grass to get out of your way. In the northeastern United States, this will usually, *but not always,* be of a harmless variety, such as a garter snake or black snake. In the southern and western states where poisonous snakes are more often found, there is a greater chance of its being dangerous.

Thus, the first rule of catching a snake is: *know positively what kind it is*. If you are uncertain, leave it alone. Check with your local science or nature museum, or collect with someone who can identify all of the local snakes.

Only a few varieties of snakes make good short-term pets. Many

The eastern milk snake, above, is a constrictor that feeds on mice and rats. Below, green (or grass) snakes emerge from their eggs. Note how the egg changes from white to clear as the snakes hatch.

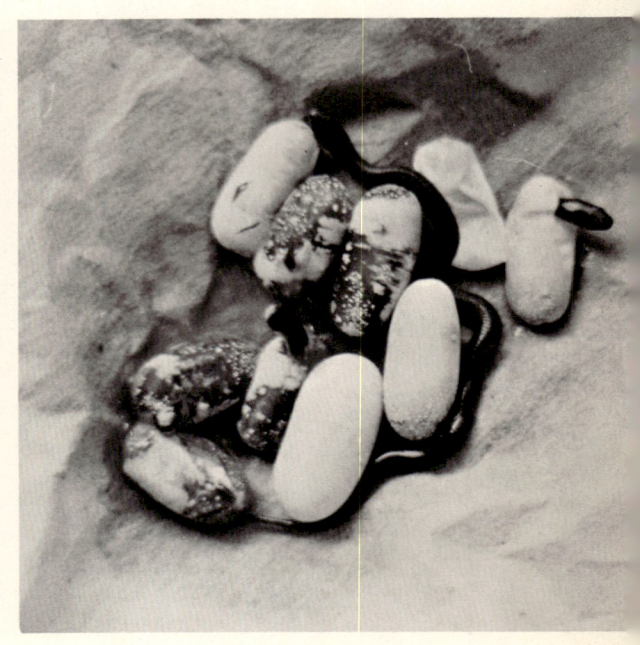

52

kinds, although harmless, will not eat in captivity or will become frightened and injure themselves by banging against their cage or terrarium. One of the best and most interesting to study is the garter snake. These are found throughout the United States, often living in grass near the edges of ponds or lakes, where they feed on frogs, insects and small fish.

One of the best ways to catch a snake — once you identify it — is with a long forked stick. Find a slim, forked tree branch and cut it about five feet long, with a two-inch fork. Approach your snake from the rear and quickly, but as gently as possible, trap him just behind the head with the fork. Then carry him home in an old pillow case or laundry bag.

A garter snake should be kept in a dry terrarium with newspaper on the bottom. Add some leaves and bark from a dead tree for the snake to hide under, a stick or two, and a bowl of water. Be sure the bowl is deep enough for the snake to put its head under the water, but heavy enough so it can't tip it over. Should the water spill, remove whatever got wet and replace it with dry materials. A snake kept in a damp place may develop a skin disease or fungus which can only be cured by releasing it in the open air and sunshine. The terrarium must have a smooth cover such as a piece of pegboard or thin plywood with small holes drilled in it for ventilation. If not covered, the snake will probably crawl out and hide in your furniture! Do not use screen wire because the snake may rub its head against the rough surface, scrape off some of its protective scales and develop infected sores. However, tree bark or a rough stick is important especially when a snake is ready to shed and needs the rough surface to "catch" the peeling skin.

The easiest foods to feed garter snakes are live earthworms, crickets and grasshoppers from your garden, or meal worms which you can grow or buy in pet shops. Snakes should be fed every two or three days, the water kept fresh, and the newspapers changed at least once a week.

Snakes should only be kept as short-term pets during the spring and summer months, then released in the early fall. When you decide to let your snake go, take it to the same area in which you caught it (or one as similar as possible) and release it. Never release a snake after the weather has dropped below fifty degrees regularly; it will be unable to hibernate and will freeze to death.

You can have fun watching your snake and will discover some interesting facts about it. Did you know that a snake can swallow food that is several times the size of its head? Watch how your snake works its jaws from side to side over the food as it swallows it, and you may be surprised to see a large lump part way down its body. If you put your snake in a flat container with sand on the bottom, you can observe how it moves. Are the lines it makes on the sand with its moving body straight or crooked? You may notice that if your snake braces itself against a side of the terrarium, its muscles can support almost the entire body length on the last inch or so of its tail.

Lizards

Lizards differ from snakes in several ways. The most obvious is that all but three of an unusual variety called "glass snakes" have legs with sharp claws that enable them to run, climb and jump every fast. Gecko lizards have suction cups on their feet, and can run across the ceiling. Lizards also have eyelids, which close from the bottom up, and ears, while snakes cannot shut their eyes nor hear sound vibrations through the air.

Because a lizard is a very fast moving animal, it is quite difficult to catch. The best way to catch one is to surprise it under a flat rock and quickly put your hand over its back, trapping it between your hand and the ground. Then slowly move your fingers together around its back and pick it up. If you spot a lizard on a fence, sidewalk or tree, get close to it by moving slowly. When you are within reach, either distract it with one hand while you catch it with the other, or move your hand slowly to within a few inches of its back and grab quickly. If you can approach a lizard from behind you have a much better chance of capturing it. Never catch a lizard by its tail, however, as the tail will usually break off in your hand and the injured lizard escape.

Three varieties called anoles, fence lizards and skinks are all fairly widespread in their ranges, although fewer lizards are found in the northeastern states than in those of the south and west. If you want to study lizards and can't catch one, you can buy them in many pet shops. The most common, and least expensive, is the anole, mistakenly called a "chameleon" because it can change color to match its surroundings. Some pet shops carry a wide variety, including the giant iguanas. In years past horned toads (which are lizards, not toads) were very popular. Today,

Lizards can be found in most areas of the United States.

however, these are protected by strict laws which prohibit their capture and sale.

Set up your lizard terrarium with a sand or dirt bottom, some tree bark, stones, and a growing plant or two. The top should be secure, and may be of screen wire, pegboard or plywood with small holes in it. Place the terrarium in a sunny spot, or put a strong lamp, such as a gooseneck desk lamp (75 to 100 watt bulb), above it. Lizards enjoy basking in hot light for hours.

Lizards feed on many kinds of insects, common house spiders, flies and meal worms. Skinks relish termites and termite eggs. Most lizards, unlike other reptiles, do not drink from standing water, but instead depend on moisture they get from their food, or dew drops they lick from leaves of plants. If you include a small pot of philodendron or ivy in the terrarium and sprinkle it lightly with water each day, the lizard will drink drops from the leaves and have a place to climb. Provide your lizard with a twig or piece of rough bark, because, like the snake, it will need something to rub against when it is ready to shed its old skin.

Try changing the color arrangement in your terrarium, particularly if you have an anole for a pet, and see how many different colors the lizard will adopt in order to blend into its surroundings. Why is this important for it to survive in the wild? Keep a record of how much your lizard eats each day and you may be surprised at the total number of meal worms, spiders, and other food it consumes. Think how many insects one lizard must eat in the wild!

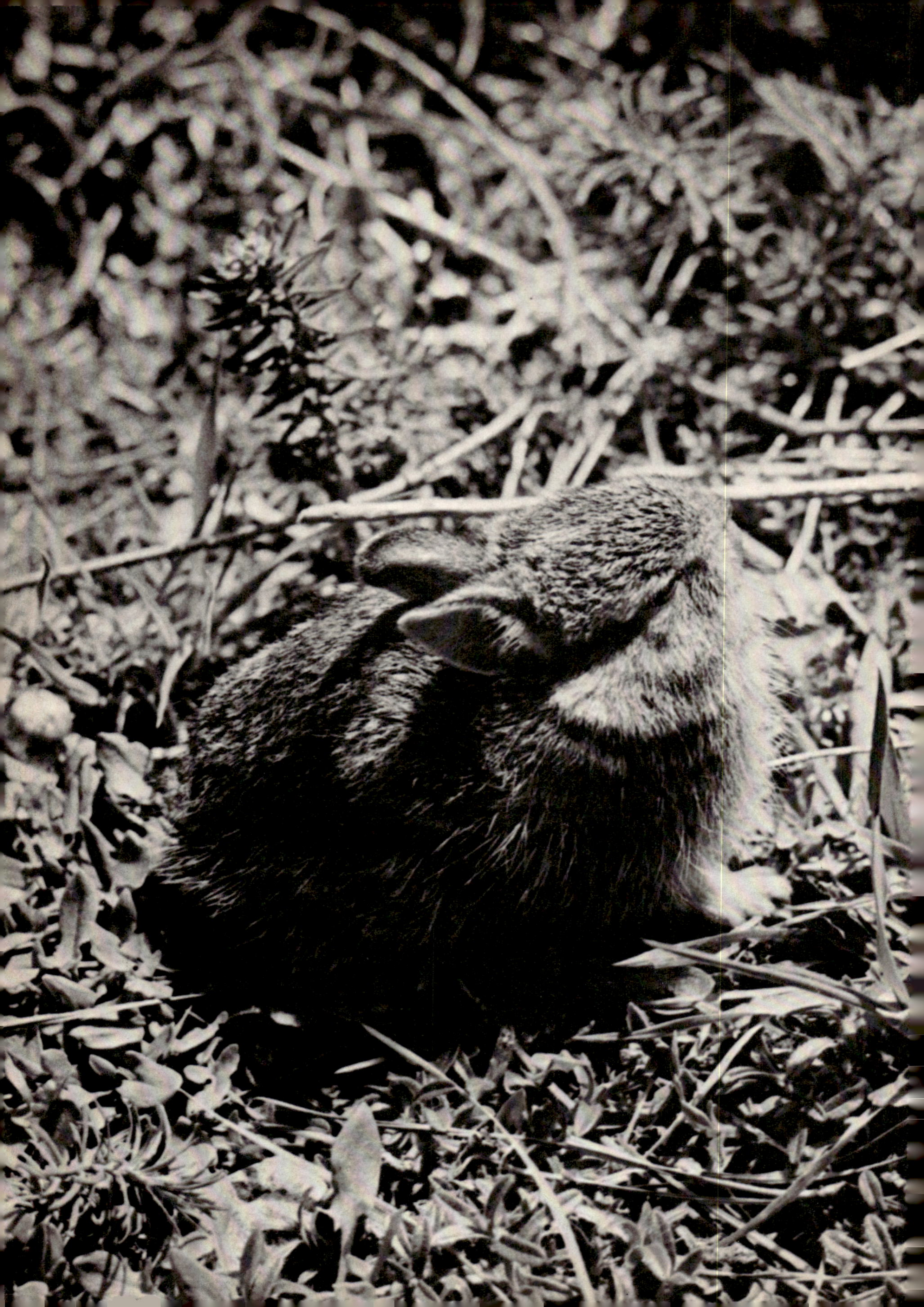

CHAPTER 7

Mammals

THE CLASS OF ANIMALS CALLED *Mammals* INCLUDES ALL ANIMALS THAT nurse their young with milk. Most mammals are fur-bearing and live on land, although a few, such as whales and porpoises, have no hair and spend their lives in the sea. Some thirty to forty different kinds of wild mammals can be found in most states of the U.S. However, aside from mice, squirrels, rabbits, chipmunks and a few others, they are seldom encountered by people because they are nocturnal or secretive.

A few wild mammals make good short-term pets; some, such as raccoons and skunks, can be domesticated and kept for several years by an experienced trainer. This chapter will tell you about some of the common mammals you may find in your yard or woods and which can be brought home safely as short-term pets. Because most mammals are protected by conservation laws (which differ from one state to another), it is important that you find out what the regulations are in your state and observe them!

NOTE: If you find an injured mammal, ask an adult to help you take it to a veterinarian, or call the nearest ASPCA or nature center for advice. DO NOT try to pick it up or comfort it unless you are certain how it should be handled.

Wild Mice

Of all the mammals you might find in the fields or around your home, wild mice are the easiest to care for, and they do well for the longest period of time in captivity. These animals nest in attics, between the

Young eastern cottontail rabbits are fun to watch as they nibble the dewy grass in early spring mornings or late afternoons.

White-footed mouse.

walls and in other cozy spots around the house, and come out at night to forage for food — often inside your kitchen cupboards! If you can capture one or two, you will have some good pets, and also please your mother by getting the mice out of her kitchen.

The most common mice which you may catch are the white-footed or deer mouse and the meadow mouse or meadow vole. You can tell them apart because the white-footed mouse has a long tail, pointed nose, and a brown head and back with white on its chest, stomach and feet, while the meadow mouse has a short tail and blunt nose, and is entirely a rich brown color.

The best home for mice is a small wire cage, such as the one described in Chapter Two, or a glass terrarium with a screen wire top. You can make a field habitat by giving the mice a dirt floor and some growing plants. Or you can give them shredded newspapers, cedar or other wood shavings, or pine needles and some cotton for bedding. Be sure to provide them with a fresh bowl of water daily and change the bedding at least once a week — preferably every two or three days.

They should also have an exercise wheel. This can be purchased at a pet shop, or you can make one fairly easily. Take a piece of strong but fairly small-mesh wire such as you might use for constructing a cage, and cut a strip twelve inches long by three inches wide. Leave the end wires sticking out. Bend the strip into as even a circle as possible, tuck the end wires under the cross wires on the opposite ends and bend around firmly with pliers. To complete your wheel, cut four pieces of heavy gauge wire about two inches longer than the diameter of your wheel. Get a heavy nail at least four inches long; take each piece of wire and bend it completely around the nail at the center of the wire. Finally, attach the ends of the four pieces of wire to the outside edges and your wheel is ready to mount. A stand can be made from two pieces of wood nailed together at right angles, or if your cage has wooden ends, simply nail the wheel firmly to one of them. If you cannot build this yourself, ask your school shop teacher to help you.

Feed your mice daily on bird seed, lettuce, bits of carrots and fig newtons; the combination of these foods gives them a well-balanced diet. Pieces of yellow cheese, nuts, and oatmeal or other cereals can also be included. Mice also need some sticks, twigs or small pieces of wood to gnaw on because their teeth grow continually and must be kept worn down. Their food should be placed in a shallow dish and any uneaten food removed before you put in fresh.

Adult wild mice can be tamed; be careful at first, however, as newly-captured mice will be afraid and probably try to bite you until they become accustomed to captivity. If you are lucky enough to catch a pregnant female who then gives birth in captivity, you can tame the babies more easily. When properly cared for, mice can live several years in captivity. If you decide to let them go, release them in a field or woods during warm months.

Squirrels

Baby squirrels that have fallen from their nests are sometimes found in yards, along sidewalks or in the woods, especially during late spring or early summer. The first thing you should do if you find one, is look for

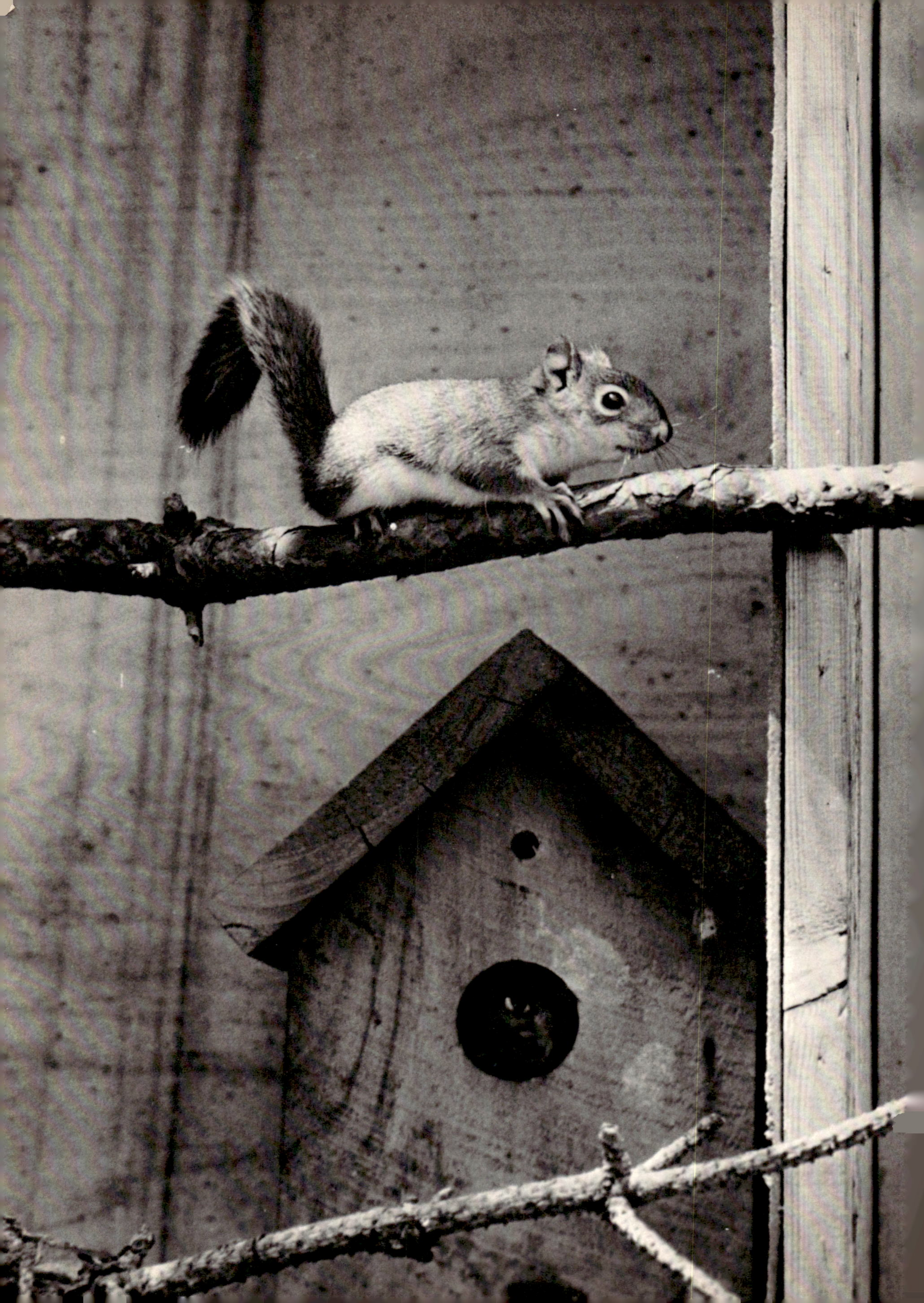

the nest, which is usually in the nearest tree. Fasten a small box or old hat to the trunk or in the branches as high as you can reach, and put the baby in it. Leave the area for a few hours, then return to see if its parents have taken it back to its nest. If not, take the orphan home and give it immediate attention.

At first, the baby will require careful attention and feeding. Make up a cage or terrarium similar to that for mice, and give the baby a nest of soft cotton, clean soft rags, sawdust or wood shavings. Put a top on the container and keep it in a warm spot. If the squirrel is very tiny and barely has its eyes open, feed it on canned baby milk, or Similac, mixed half and half with water at room temperature. Put the mixture in an eyedropper and try to feed the baby. You will probably have to feed it every hour or so, with a heavy feeding at night and first thing in the morning. When it is old enough to eat by itself, you can start offering it bits of raw vegetables, sunflower seeds and nuts, as well as sticks or pieces of wood on which to gnaw.

As the squirrel grows and becomes lively, give it an exercise wheel similar to that made for wild mice and, later, let it go outside. If you continue to offer it food in one spot of your yard each day, you will find you have a new backyard friend and you will also help the squirrel become accustomed to living in the wild.

Rabbits

Baby rabbits, just as baby squirrels, are sometimes found abandoned or lost in yards and fields. Again, as with a baby squirrel, try to locate the nest and return it; or if you uncover a nest by accident, cover the babies and leave them. The mother will usually return. If a baby is brought home uninjured by your cat or dog, however, you must try to give it proper care.

The care for a very tiny rabbit is the same as that required by a baby squirrel, except that it will need a larger cage or a box with a wire top. As it grows stronger and can eat by itself from a bowl, you can give it strained baby food vegetables, especially carrots, and gradually introduce shredded lettuce and raw carrots.

The rabbit should be released outdoors as soon as it begins to run around and becomes quite frisky.

A family of red squirrels have set up housekeeping in an abandoned bird house.

Raccoons

Because raccoons have less fear of humans than most other wild animals, they live close to built-up areas and may be seen at night in suburban streets, or heard rattling the tops of garbage pails for food. Many females are killed along the highways and, in the spring, they may have one or more young huddled pitifully against them. Other lost or orphaned young raccoons may simply wander into your yard.

These animals are very intelligent, and can be raised by older children who are willing to devote consistent care and attention to a difficult job. Some states, however, prohibit the capture of raccoons and most others require a special permit to keep them. Thus, you must first ask your local game warden or nearest nature center about your state laws and requirements before deciding to raise a raccoon.

Once you have determined that you *may* raise a raccoon, you then must decide if you *can* care for one properly. Raising a baby raccoon is as much, if not more, trouble as raising a human baby! You will spend so much time with it and the raccoon will respond with such affection, that gradually it will seem like a member of your family.

Having found a baby raccoon and, after careful thought, decided to try raising it, the first thing you must do is give it a warm, comfortable temporary home. Start with a deep cardboard box, line the bottom with newspaper, and give the raccoon an old pair of flannel pajamas or other clean cloth for a bed. This is the only easy step!

A very young raccoon must be fed milk from a bottle until it refuses to eat this way. Canned baby milk or Similac mixed with an equal amount of water plus a drop or two of Karo Syrup must be fed every two or three hours if the raccoon is very small. This means feeding it before you go to bed and getting up twice in the middle of the night until the raccoon is strong enough to survive the night without extra feedings. If you think you can get away with not feeding it during the night when you first take it home, you have a lesson to learn about raccoons. It will scream and carry on until you get out of bed and give it the formula. This can take a half hour or more and by the time you have crawled back into bed it will seem as though it is screaming again five minutes later. The first few nights you can give the baby the companionship of a substitute brother or sister by putting a hot water bottle wrapped in soft cloth and filled with warm (not hot) water, in its box or by placing a ticking clock near it. The warmth of the hot water bottle and the sound of the clock give it security and you may get some sleep!

Another problem frequently encountered with a baby raccoon is that it may not be able to eliminate wastes by itself. If this occurs, you must hold the baby over the toilet after each feeding and rub its stomach gently with a warm sponge until you are sure it is comfortable. It is most important to sterilize the sponge by boiling it after each use so that germs are kept away from the orphan. Its box must also be kept clean by changing the paper and bedding several times each day.

As soon as your raccoon will accept strained baby food from an eye dropper, start to feed it as much mixed vegetables and custard as it will consume. All young raccoons like custard, and by mixing vegetables with the custard, you can get them to eat both. Gradually it will begin to eat out of a dish and you will then be able to substitute table scraps for baby foods.

As your raccoon grows and the box is no longer adequate as a sleeping place, you will need to build a cage for it outside. Raccoons like plenty of freedom, so the cage should be at least four feet square by ten feet high. One of the best cages is made with cedar posts for the uprights and crossbars and heavy turkey-wire mesh strung around the frame. A lock must be placed on the door as raccoons soon learn to open ordinary latches or bolts. The bottom of the cage should be a few feet off the ground to prevent your pet from getting damp or from being bothered by parasites. A nesting box made from an old nail keg with some wood shavings in it and placed upon two or three posts near the top of the cage will give the raccoon the feeling it is sleeping in the security of a tree. Be sure it has a small galvanized tub of clean water at all times.

By the time you have gone through all the problems of raising the baby, labored to build a large enough cage and grown very fond of your pet, you must still give serious consideration to the raccoon's future. These animals can live to be ten years old. Unless you intend to care for a raccoon during its lifetime, you should release it when it is about six months old. If you turn it loose near your house, you can continue to put food outside until the raccoon learns to fend for itself. You may also offer it to a nature center, but such centers are usually given many more

NEXT PAGE: This four-month old orphan raccoon will soon be ready to return to the wild.

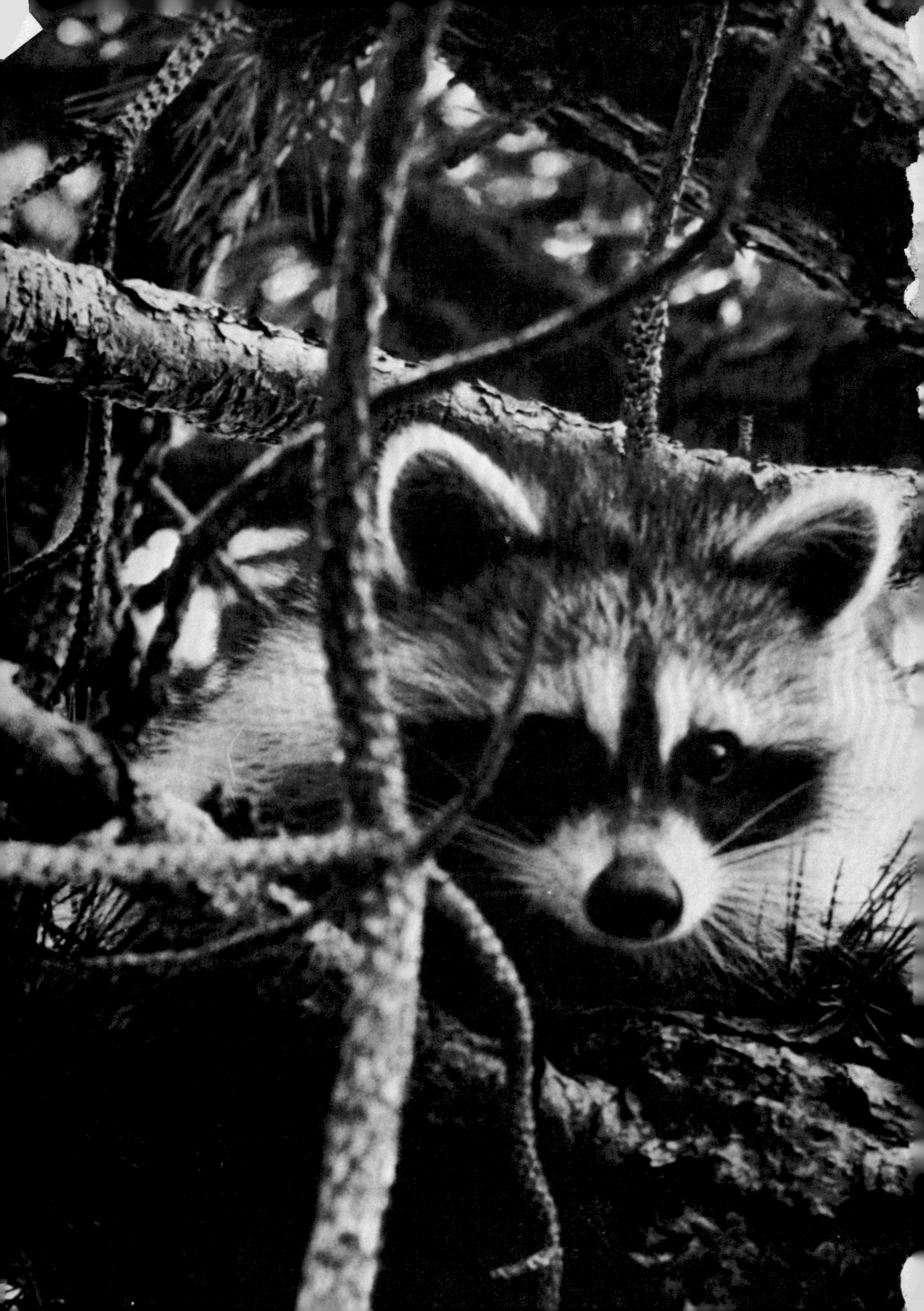

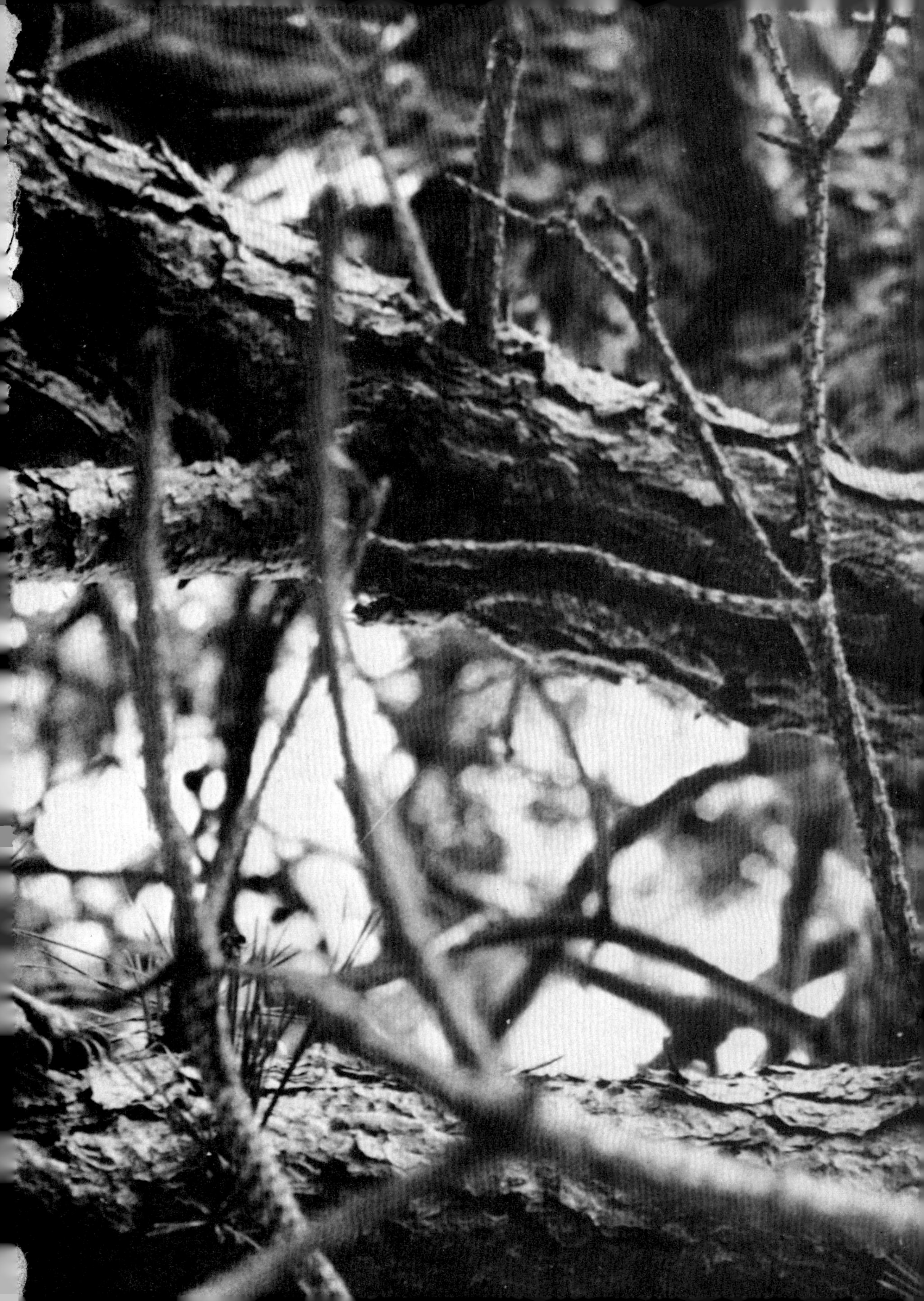

animals each spring than they can care for and thus may not be able to accept it.

Skunks

Like raccoons, these animals *can* be raised in captivity, but state and local laws frequently prohibit their capture. Thus, you should check with your local warden or nature center, before deciding to raise a skunk.

A baby skunk, if found beside its dead mother or wandering in your yard, should first be taken to a veterinarian to be checked for rabies. *If, and only if,* you seriously wish to keep it as a pet for its life span — some

A skunk without its scent is defenseless. *(Photo by Mary Eastman)*

seven to ten years — the veterinarian can also remove its musk or scent glands. Once they have lost their spray, skunks are defenseless in the wild and should only be turned over to a zoo or nature center if you later change your mind. On the other hand, you can raise a scented skunk from a baby and then release it in the wild as soon as it becomes an adult. They will not spray you, provided you are gentle with them as babies and allow them to gain confidence in you as a friend. If you have more than one skunk, however, keep them outdoors because they will have family quarrels and spray each other!

A baby skunk requires the same attention and feeding schedule as a baby raccoon. When it is very young it must be fed small amounts of diluted condensed milk with a few drops of Karo syrup out of a nursing bottle or eye dropper every three or four hours. As it grows older, introduce leftover meats and vegetables from your table, and gradually wean it away from the bottle. When fully grown, a skunk requires only one meal per day.

These few — wild mice, squirrels and rabbits, and sometimes raccoons or skunks — are about the only wild mammals recommended as possible pets in the home. People trained as zoologists or experienced at animal handling have successfully raised many others. But unless you have such training, you are more likely to do harm, both to the animals and yourself, by attempting to raise any of them.

In the last chapter you will find a discussion of four other wild mammals — gerbils, hamsters, guinea pigs and flying squirrels — which can also make excellent pets and which are usually found in pet shops. It is best to try your hand at caring for one of these before you consider keeping any mammal that comes directly from the fields or woods.

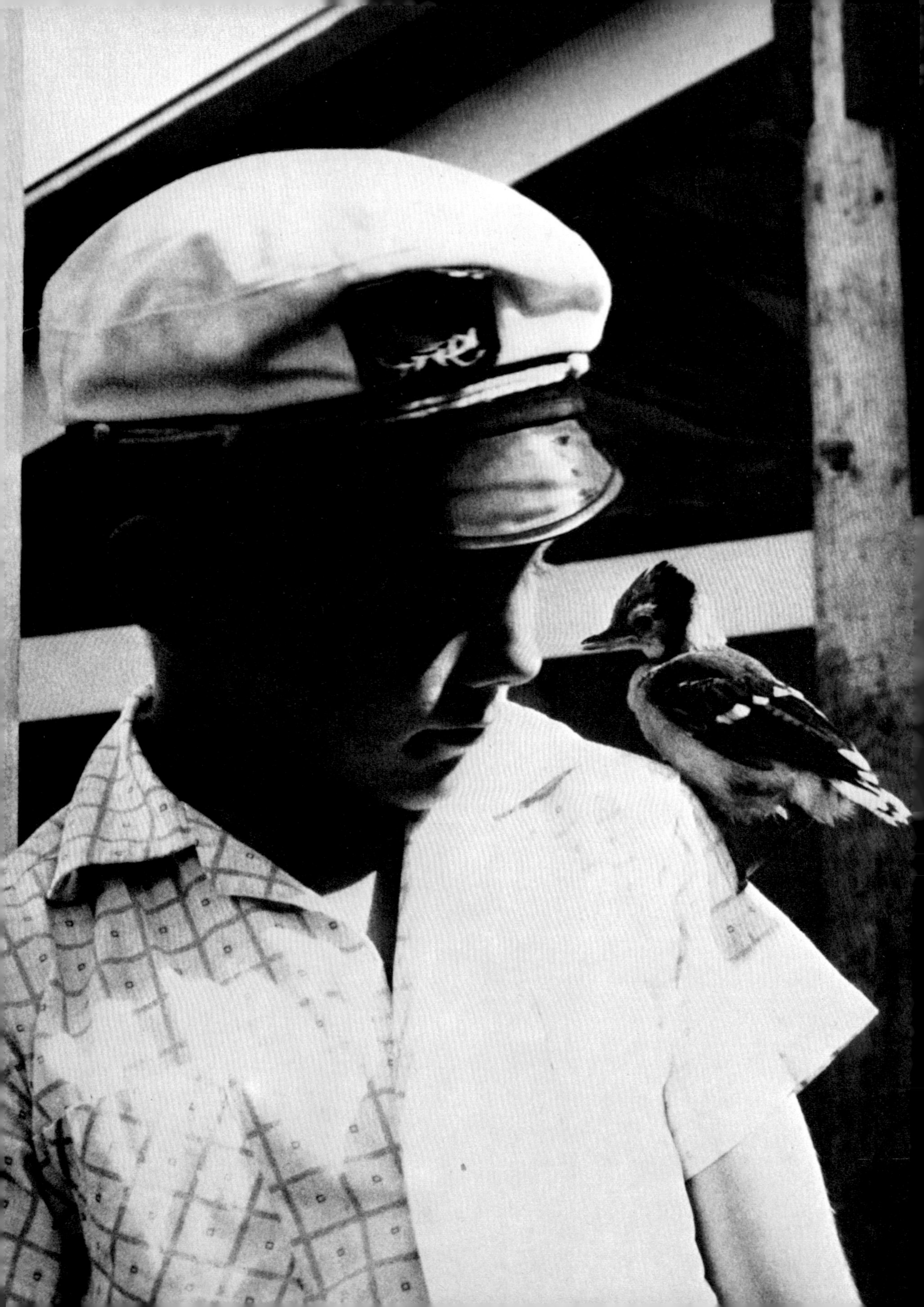

CHAPTER 8

Wild Birds

IF THE VIEW THROUGH YOUR WINDOW IS DRAB AND DULL DURING WINTER months, why not bring wild birds to your yard to add life, color and entertainment? The only trick to attracting wild birds is to keep a feeder well supplied with seed and/or suet. Start early in the fall so the birds will adopt your yard as their feeding grounds; then feed them regularly all winter because they will come to depend upon your daily handout.

Besides entertainment, you can also turn your bird feeder into a very interesting study project by learning to identify your visitors. Your local bookstore or nature center have inexpensive bird guides for sale that show you drawings or photographs of the most common birds. Buy one of these and see how many birds you can identify.

If you want to make a long study, perhaps one that will be acceptable as a school science project, start a "checklist." This is a daily listing of the birds you see, whether they are males or females, how often they appear and under what weather conditions. A typical checklist for the northeastern states is shown on the following page; your checklist will vary, depending upon your location, the season and, most important, your ability to observe carefully and regularly.

As you progress with your project, you will acquire more and more skill at identifying birds. At first you may only know one or two common ones when you see them close up. Gradually, as you become acquainted with their looks, habits and ways of flying, you will be able to distinguish

A young Naturalist gets acquainted with a young bluejay.

YOUR NAME: Kim Harris	LOCALITY: Back Yard
DATE: Sept. 26, 1970	WEATHER: Cloudy + cool

SPECIES:	NO. OF MALES:	NO. OF FEMALES:
Purple Finch	1	2
Chickadee	5	
Cardinal	1	1
House-Sparrow	2	2

a certain bird in flight or perched on a tree top. Finally, after you have learned the common birds, you may be surprised to see a new species arrive. Your chances of spotting a rare bird in your neighborhood are as good as anyone else's. And very much better if you can identify it!

Feeders

Bird feeders are easy to build, or they can be purchased in many hardware stores, pet shops or woodworking shops. The simplest feeder is a wooden tray nailed on supports to the outside of your window or in a tree. A roof, seed holder and perches will be welcome additions. Another practical feeder is illustrated at the opening of this chapter; you can probably think of many more designs.

Be sure to place feeders close to shrubs and trees so the birds can fly into the branches for protection and shelter. When your feeder is installed, put in a variety of food to suit the tastes of different birds. Packaged seed mixtures, especially those containing millet, hemp and sunflower seeds, provide the best assortment. Small seed-eaters like cracked corn and peanut hearts as well as sunflower seeds; finches go for thistle seed.

Beef suet, which you can probably get from your butcher at no charge, is another favorite of many birds. You can pack this in a plastic bag that has holes in it, a small net or similar holder and hang it from a tree branch near the seed feeder. You can also drill holes in a twelve inch long small log or four by four and pack them with a mixture of suet and grain or seeds. Insert pegs for perches below the holes, and hang it from a branch. Make certain that any wire or metal parts of any feeder are dipped in paraffin. If the moist eye of a bird comes into contact with freezing uncoated metal, the eye can be seriously damaged or destroyed.

Birds also need water throughout the winter. Although they can usually find rain water or melted snow, you can help them by keeping a water dish in your yard. Use a plastic or rubber container that will not break if it freezes. In extreme periods of cold weather, a drop or two of glycerine in the water will prevent it from freezing and will not harm the birds.

Bird Houses

In the spring some of the birds you have fed all winter will be looking for a place to nest. The number of different places and sizes of nesting space required is almost as large as the number of species of birds around your yard. Some like high tree tops or under your eaves; others, low bushes or even the ground. Thus, before building a bird house you must have some idea of the species of bird most likely to use it. The following chart was developed by the Audubon Society of Connecticut, and will give you a good guideline:

BIRD HOUSE DIMENSION CHART

Species	Floor of cavity	Depth of cavity	Entrance above floor	Diameter of entrance	Height above ground
	Inches	Inches	Inches	Inches	Feet
Bluebird	5 x 5	8	6	1½	5-10
Robin	6 x 8	8	(3 sides open)		6-15
Chickadee	4 x 4	8-10	6-8	1⅛	6-15
Titmouse	4 x 4	8-10	6-8	1¼	6-15
Nuthatch	4 x 4	8-10	6-8	1¼	12-20
House Wren	4 x 4	6-8	1-6	1	6-10
Tree Swallow	5 x 5	6	1-5	1½	10-15
Purple Martin	6 x 6	6	1	2½	15-20
Crested Flycatcher	6 x 6	8-10	6-8	2	8-20
Flicker	7 x 7	16-18	14-16	2½	6-20
Downy Woodpecker	4 x 4	8-10	6-8	1¼	6-20
Screech Owl	8 x 8	12-15	9-12	3	10-30
Sparrow Hawk	8 x 8	12-15	9-12	3	10-30
Wood Duck	10 x 18	10-24	12-16	4	10-30

If you have kept a checklist, you will immediately know which birds inhabit your neighborhood, and can build a bird house to suit the species that interests you most. If you are uncertain about the species, a house 4 x 4 inches, with a 1¼-inch entrance hole 6 to 8 inches above the floor and hung about 10 feet above the ground is a good average to attract some small common birds. Do not use metal, such as tin cans, for bird houses because the sun will make them too hot inside and the babies may die.

Most birds like to nest in privacy; once a family is established in a house, the parents will drive away other birds of the same species who come too close. For this reason you should build "single family" bird houses, with one exception. The only common "apartment dweller" is the purple martin. If these are found around your area, try designing a multi-floored bird house, each unit being a 6-cubic inch space with a 2½-inch diameter entrance one inch above the floor.

Bird houses should be built in such a way that you can remove the roofs to clean them after each season's nesting, and should have small (¼-inch) holes drilled in one corner of the floors to drain off any water that leaks in. They can be made from pine or plywood boards and painted with a protective paint, or from cedar boards that will withstand weather for many years.

Caring for Injured and Orphan Birds

Nearly everyone, at one time or another, has found a sick or injured bird and wondered how to help it.

If the bird is a baby which has fallen from a nest but appears healthy, you should first attempt to locate the nest and return the fledgling. If the nest is too high, place or fasten a cigar box or an old hat in the tree as high as you can reach, then put the baby in it. Chances are good that after you go away, the parents will come to the rescue. If not, you are in charge of the orphan.

Place the baby in an artificial nest made of soft paper such as Kleenex, toilet paper or paper toweling. A shoe box or similar size container will serve as the "bird house". Put it in a warm, dry part of your house as young birds are highly susceptible to chills and respiratory infections. The paper nesting must be changed frequently to keep it clean and free of droppings. In the wild, parent birds carry away the droppings of the young, which are called "fecal sacs".

Baby birds in general require a diet rich in protein. In the wild, the main source of protein is insects, and you may be able to provide some of these. If not, liver, kidney, lean hamburger or dog food cut into pieces will do very well. Hard boiled eggs, when mashed with milk to form a paste, make a desirable food supplement rich in protein, fat and vitamins. When the bird is very young, the mother helps the baby swallow its

NEXT PAGE: A house wren being fed a piece of suet on a long artist's paint brush.

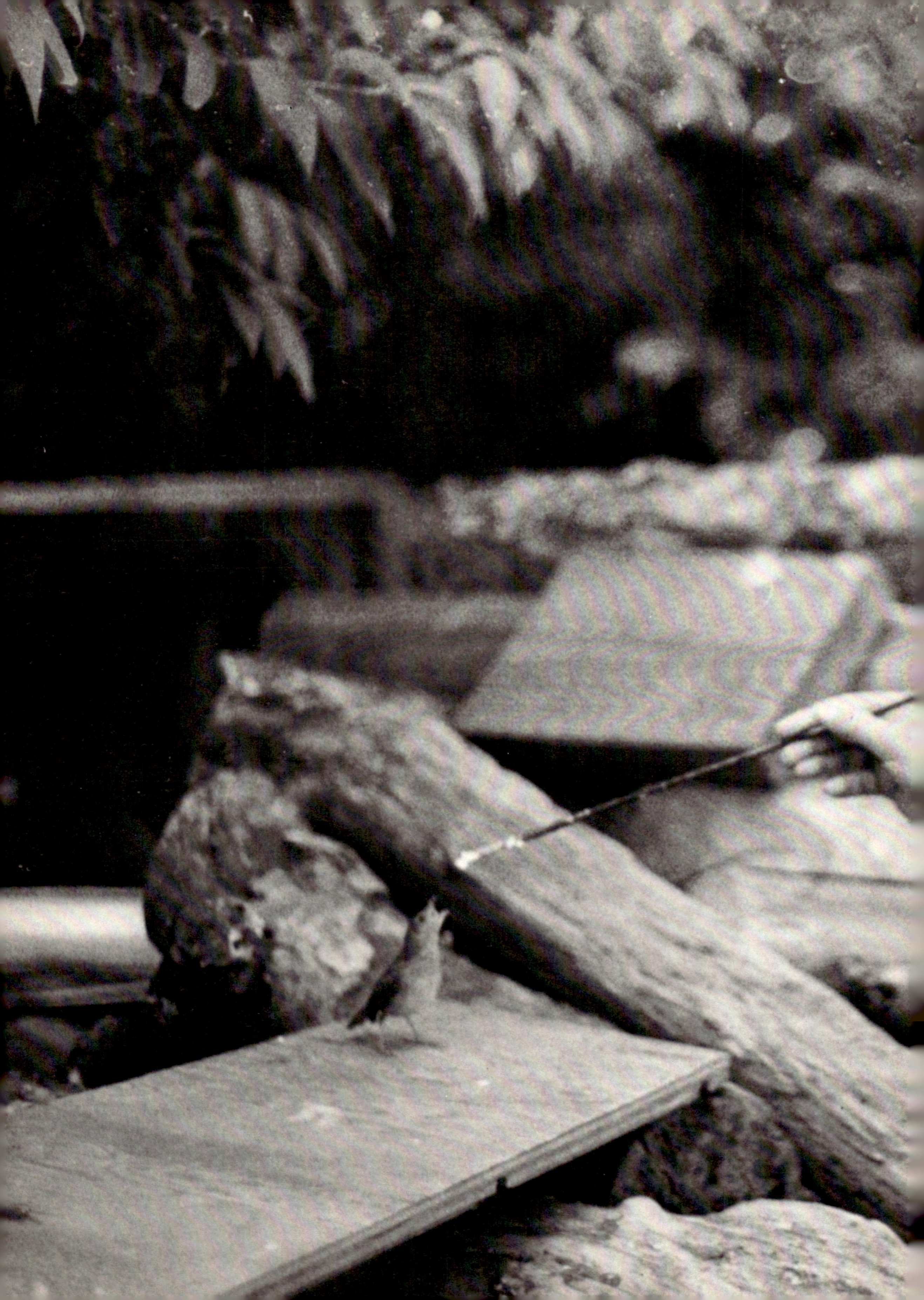

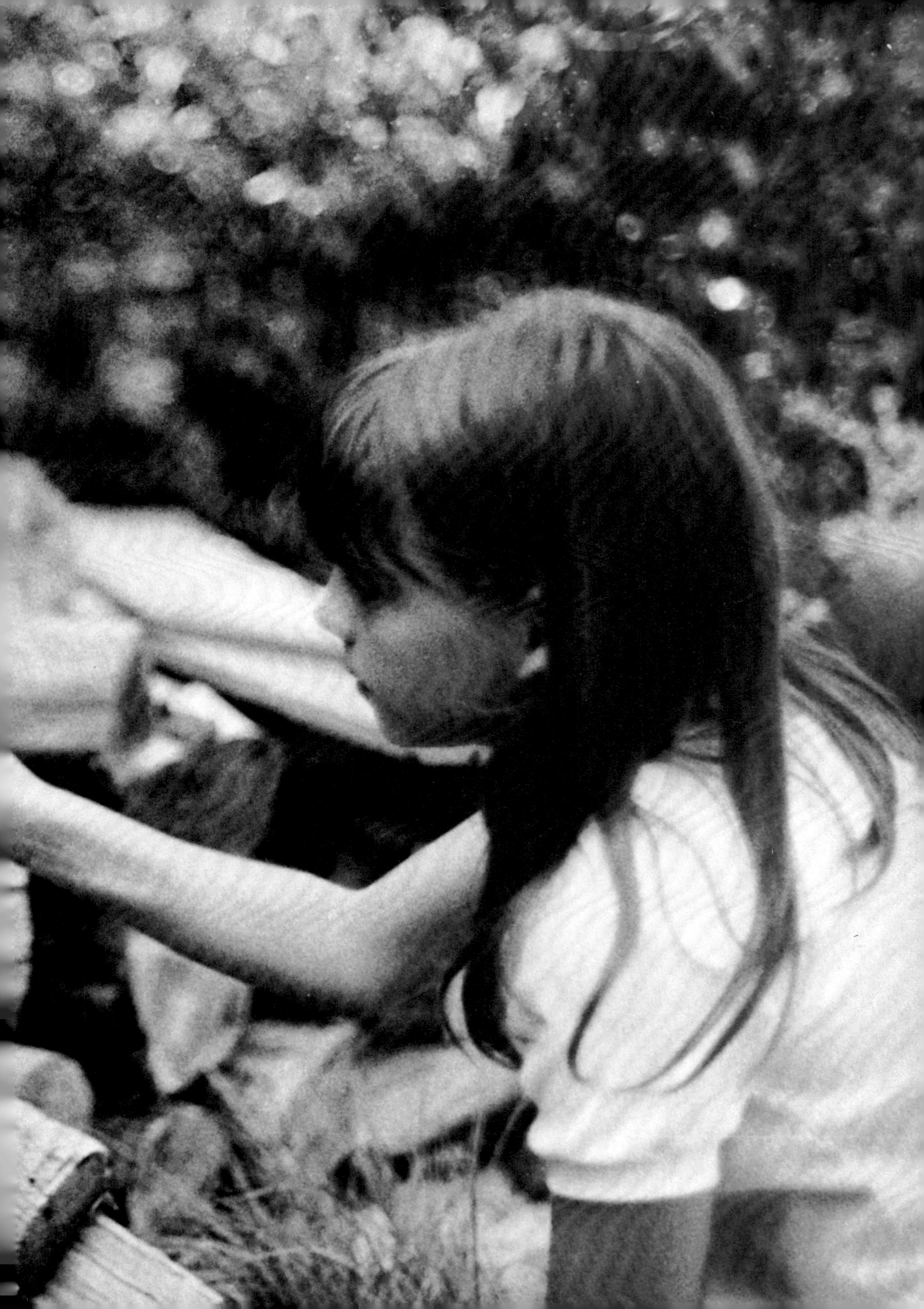

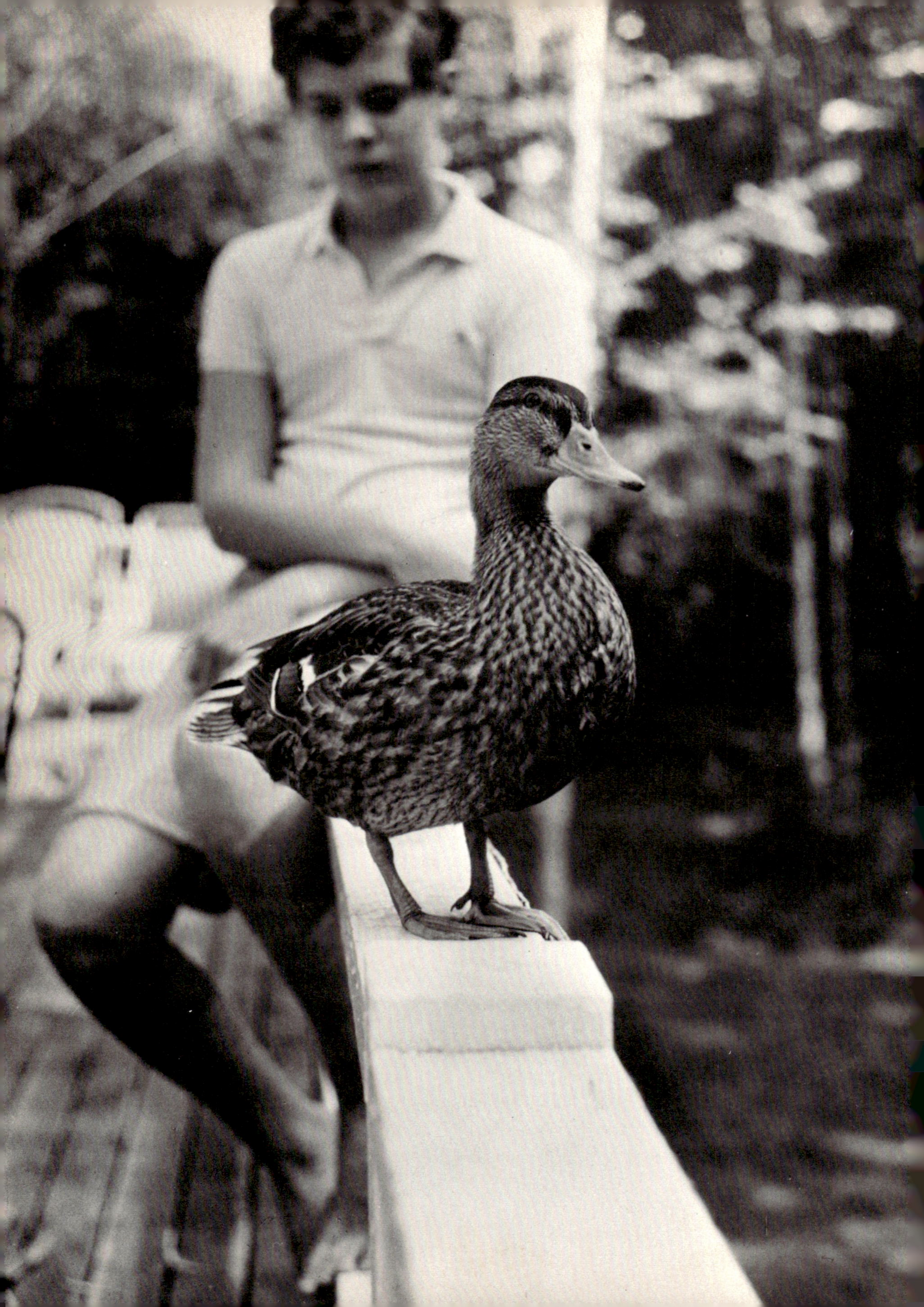

OPPOSITE PAGE: This female mallard was hatched in a school project from an egg carried home by a dog. Later the duck was raised as a family pet until old enough to fly off and find its way back to the flock. BELOW: A nest of black duck's eggs. The mother has plucked soft feathers from her body to line the edges.

food by catching it, partially eating it, and regurgitating the softened food into the fledgling's mouth. Gradually, as it grows older, the young bird learns to eat whole insects as well as seed, and finally flies off to catch its own supply.

If you should take in a baby duck, you must give it special attention. Young ducks can be very difficult to keep, and a few basic facts and rules should be followed. Use a cardboard box with papers in the bottom and place a gooseneck lamp in one corner. A light is very important for keeping your baby duck warm and secure. Food should consist of chicken mash, chopped lettuce, cooked spaghetti (chopped) and chopped hard boiled eggs. Feed your duck as much as it will eat twice each day. Offer it water in a shallow dish but not enough so that the duck can get soaked. Never put a young duck in water for a swim as this can be very harmful if it gets soaked through to the skin. As your duck begins to replace its fluff with feathers, you can give it a small container in which to swim. Pond water and plants that contain insects and insect larvae are excellent at this stage of its growth. Remember to change the papers in the box every day to keep your duck healthy. When you are ready to release your duck try to find a stream or pond frequented by people where it will have a chance to adjust slowly (or at a local park or zoo). Releasing it in a wild pond may result in its death.

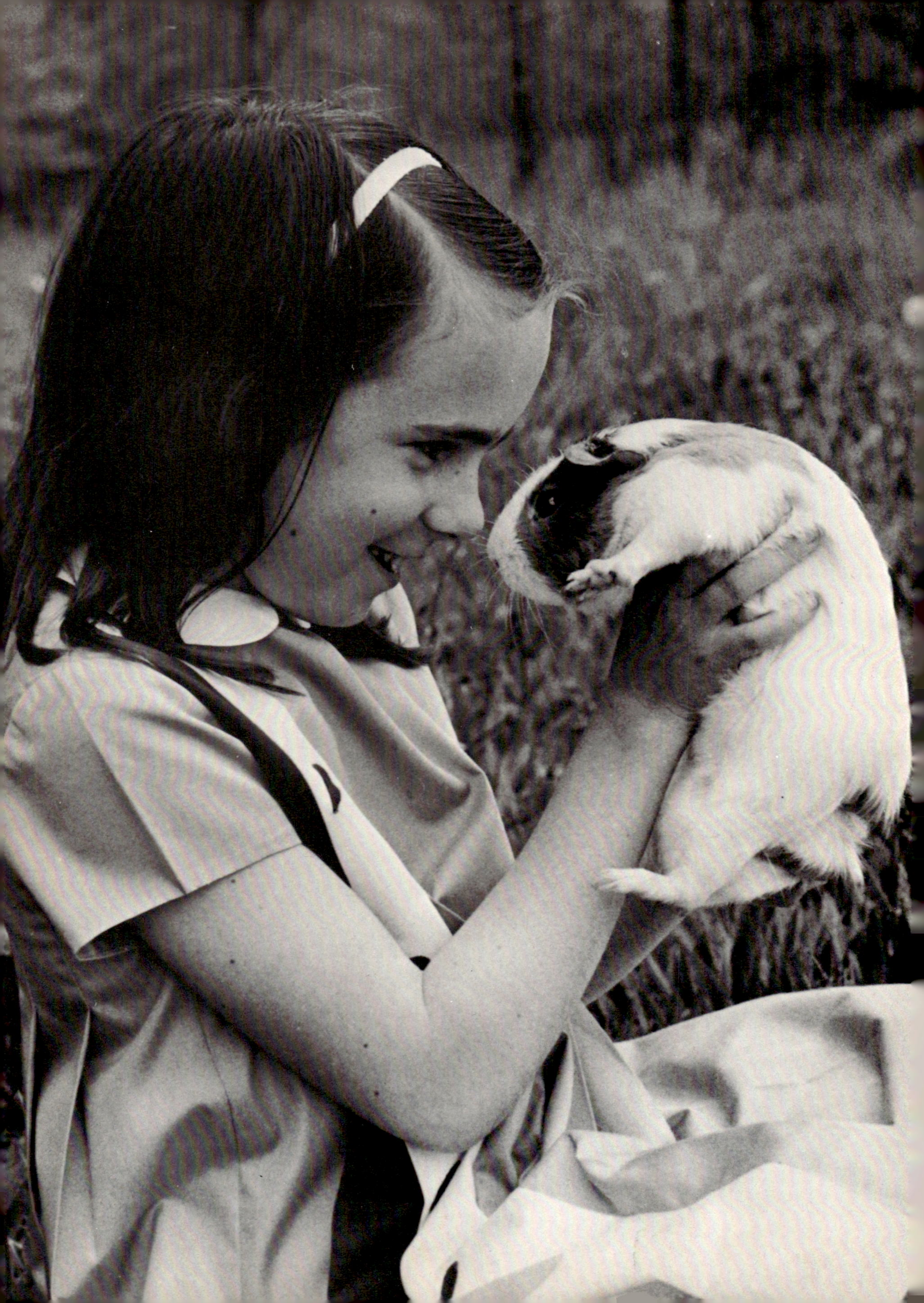

CHAPTER 9

Pet Shop Animals

So far we have considered animals you will usually find in the wild, although some of these, such as mice, can also be bought in pet shops. Other non-domesticated animals which you can buy and which make excellent pets include tropical fish, flying squirrels, guinea pigs, hamsters and gerbils. In addition to these, some pet shops carry an assortment of "exotic" or rare creatures such as boa constrictors, hawks, owls, monkeys, iguana lizards and many more. Like the majority of wild mammals, these creatures can be properly kept by experienced teenagers or adults, but should not be brought home by or for beginners.

Also in this category are the ducklings, chicks and baby rabbits often sold by pet and department stores and elsewhere at Easter time. Frequently these animals are brought home as surprises for young children only to die a short time later from neglect or improper care. Even under the proper conditions and with the best intentions, ducks and chickens are messy to keep at home and there is always the problem of what to do with them when they are no longer wanted as pets.

One way in which you can be a "young conservationist" is by not purchasing foreign or exotic animals or animals endangered with extinction. You can do your share to preserve these and other rare creatures by not buying them and by helping others to understand why they should be preserved. If you seriously want to study one of them, you should first

Fortunately, Guinea pigs are unlikely to bite. *(Photo by Mary Eastman)*

find out from books or a nature center what is involved; be certain you can care for it properly and that what you are doing is in your (and the animal's) best interests.

Tropical Fish

People of all ages enjoy collecting, studying and breeding tropical fish; they could become a hobby that you will pursue all through your life.

The basic equipment to set up a tropical fish aquarium can be inexpensive; a ten-gallon rectangular tank, water heater, thermometer, some fine gravel and plants are a good start. If you are able to add an air pump and hood light, you will have all that is required for most fish.

Set your aquarium on a strong table or stand out of direct sunlight. Wash the tank and gravel with warm water. Spread the gravel in the tank to a depth of one to two inches and, if you wish to be decorative, slope it down from back to front or form high and low spots. Then place a sheet of paper on top of the gravel so that when you add water, the gravel will not be washed out of place. Slowly pour in about half a tank-full of water, remove the paper and add your plants. You can make an attractive arrangement by placing the tallest plants toward the back and the smaller ones in the valleys and toward the front. Finally, fill the tank to within an inch or two from the top.

Now attach your thermometer and water heater, setting the heater to between 70° and 75° Fahrenheit. You will probably have to wait several hours before you can get a correct reading on the thermometer. If necessary, keep adjusting the water heater until the water stabilizes at the temperature you want. You should wait *at least* forty-eight hours before putting any fish in your aquarium; it is best to wait a week or more to let the plants take firm root.

The acid or alkaline content of your water is an important factor to tropical fish and the balance of these elements varies from one place to another. If there is a significant difference between the water in the pet store tanks and that of your tank at home, you may lose some of your fish because of the change. If you take a sample of your water with you when you first go to buy your tank, the dealer will test it for you. He can then sell you the proper chemicals to adjust your water at home.

Take your time deciding what fish you wish to buy. On your first trip to the store, get the equipment and look over the many kinds of fish. Chances are, you will want more than you can afford and you would also overcrowd the aquarium. Before buying tropical fish you should also make certain that the pet store has healthy specimens. A few bad signs are readily visible: one or two dead fish in the tank, white spots or fungus on the sides of some fish, split fins, and fish that "shimmy" or roll over in a sluggish way.

Tropical fish that lay eggs are usually more colorful and vigorous than the live-bearing fish. Some of the common egg-layers are Neon Tetras, Cardinal Tetras, Head- and Taillights, Zebra Danios, Kissing Gouramis, Penguins, and White Cloud Mountain Fish. The livebearers include Guppies, Moons, Mollies, Swordtails and Platies. Catfish or other bottom-dwelling fish are extremely important to the proper balance of your aquarium; they are scavengers that clean up food dropped to the bottom by other fish. Unless you have an air pump to add extra oxygen to the water, you should limit yourself to about twenty fish of mixed sizes and types for a ten-gallon tank. A good selection of fish that will live well together is:

2 small Catfish	2 Penguins	2 Kissing Gouramis
2 Neon Tetras	2 Swordtails	2 Guppies
3 Cardinal Tetras	3 Zebra Danios	2 White Cloud Mountain Fish

Since your new fish are very sensitive to changes in water temperature, it is important that you place them, while still in the pet store container, into the aquarium for at least 15 minutes, before you release them into the water. This enables the temperature in their temporary container to become the same as the aquarium water and the fish will not be shocked by a sudden change.

With a minimum of care, you can now enjoy your tropical fish aquarium for a long time. Feed your fish flake dry food, frozen daphnia or brine shrimp; your pet store may also suggest other prepared foods for your particular kinds of fish. They can be fed twice a day, but never give them more than they can eat in five minutes.

When the water level in the tank drops, add more to bring it back up. You should "age" this water, however, before adding it by leaving it in an open container for a few days. Siphon out any dirt that collects on

NEXT PAGE: An aquarium of tropical moons.

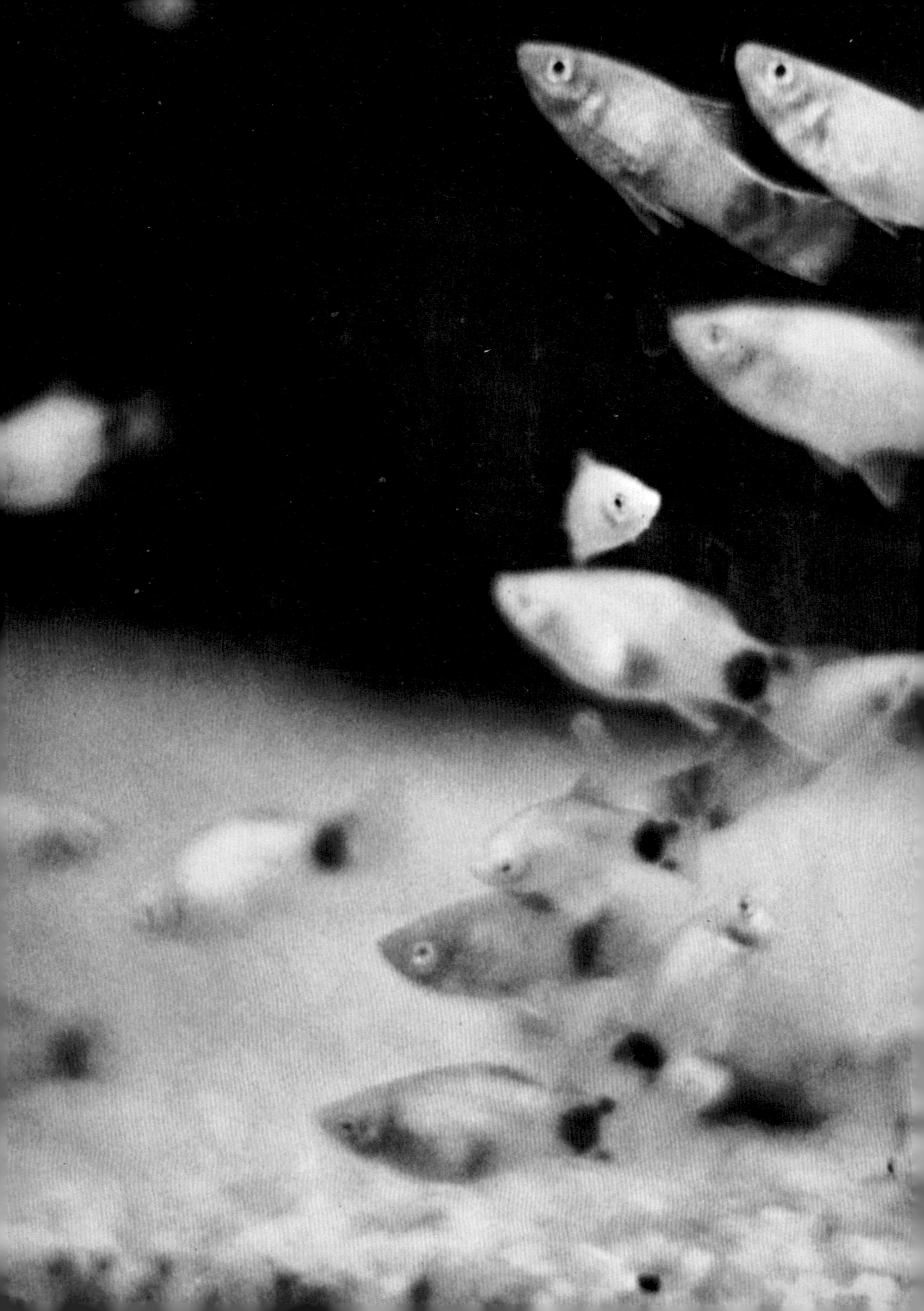

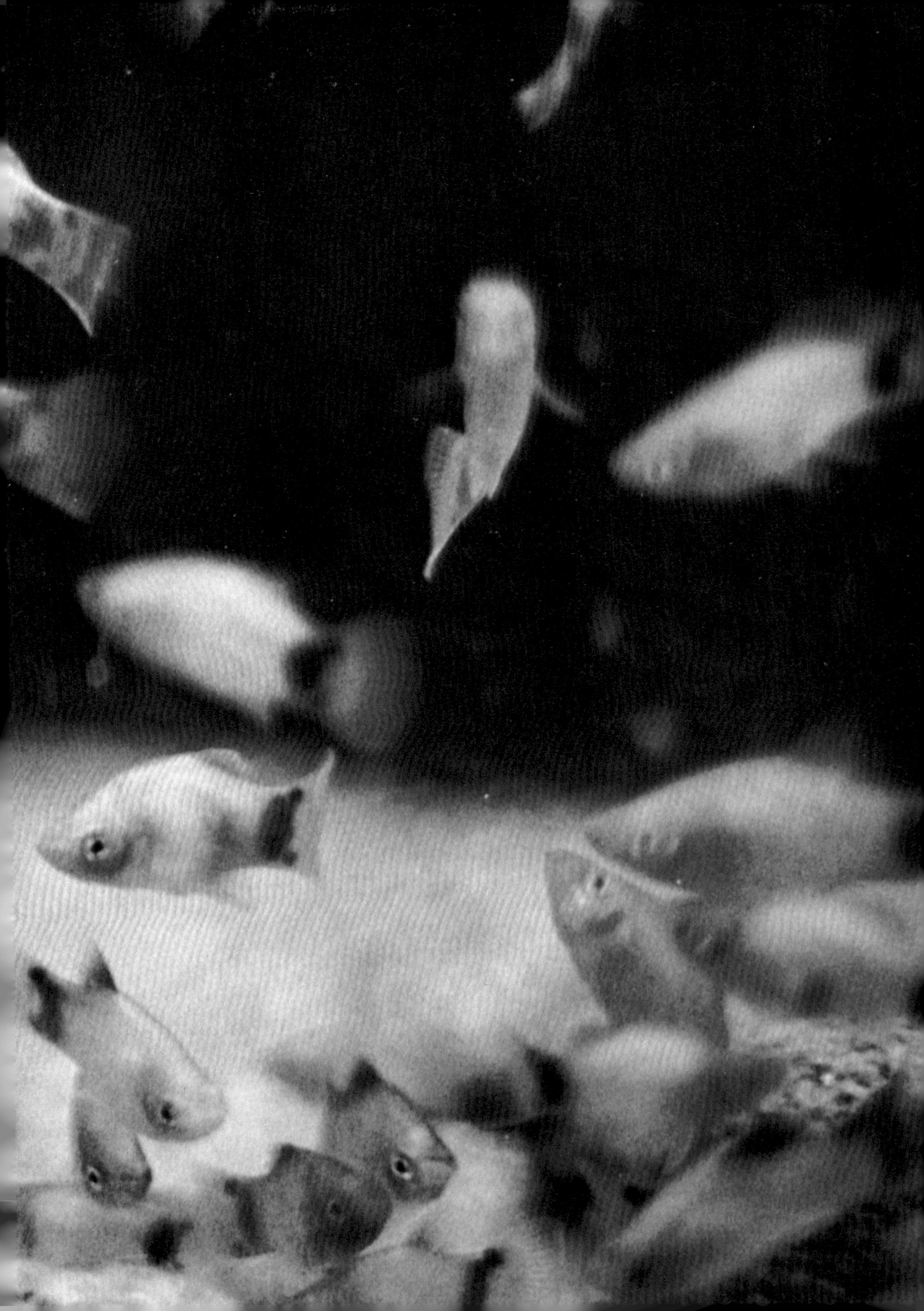

the bottom and clean the sides of the tank occasionally with a small wire brush.

Flying Squirrels

These affectionate little animals can make wonderful pets. They are clean and healthy and require a minimum of care. If possible, buy a pair of young flying squirrels; one by itself can become quite lonely and older, mature squirrels are difficult to tame.

Known as "gliders", flying squirrels do not really fly in the same sense as birds. They have extra folds of skin between their front and rear legs which, when spread, enable them to jump from a perch and glide through the air as far as thirty feet before landing on another object or on the ground. They are nocturnal creatures and thus you will seldom see them in the woods. However, if you exercise tame flying squirrels during the late afternoon and early evening, they will adjust to the schedule you choose.

It is important to give them a fairly large cage — at least three feet high and long by two feet wide. A hollow log about two feet long by six or eight inches in diameter makes an excellent nesting spot for the squirrels. Stand it on end in one corner of the cage and secure it with wire. If you cannot find a suitable log, a bird house attached to the top of a short log will serve as a substitute. Put some clean, soft rags or cedar chips inside for bedding.

Flying squirrels thrive on a diet of various kinds of nuts (especially Filberts) daily and orange or grapefruit sections once a week. You can also feed them sunflower seeds, lettuce, apple slices and similar food. Fasten an animal bottle to the side of their cage and keep it full of fresh water. Once a week add a few drops of lime water to prevent them from catching "cage paralysis" or loss of leg movement.

These animals can almost be "housebroken". Once they are accustomed to their cage, they will select a corner of it for their bathroom facilities and continue to use this one spot. Keep the area clean and covered with newspaper.

Handle your pet squirrels gently and let them come to you for food. If you give them the freedom of a room to exercise, you will find that they enjoy curling up in the pocket of a convenient coat or a favorite

Flying squirrels need a large cage and a house in which to rest.

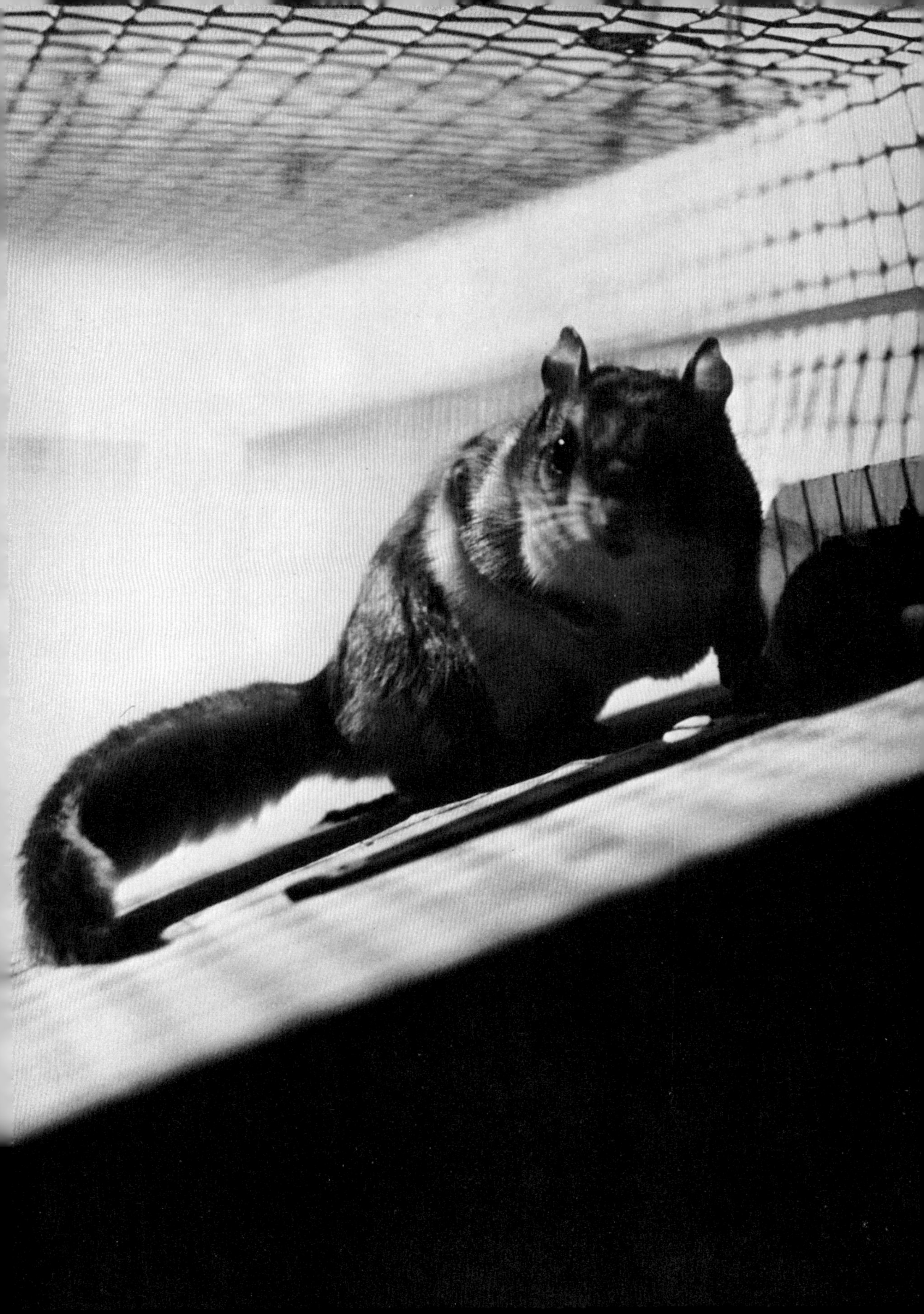

shirt. In the spring, if you have a pair, you may be surprised to find yourself with a litter of up to six babies!

Guinea pigs and hamsters

Of all the wild animals from pet shops, these two are probably the most familiar. They are healthy, easily handled, have individual personalities and can be kept in a small cage if they are given frequent exercising in a room. Guinea pigs, while slightly larger, have a more gentle nature and are less likely to bite small children.

Their basic needs are simple: a small wire cage about two feet long by one foot high and wide, bedding, a water bottle and food. Crushed sugar cane, hay or cedar chips are good bedding; a piece of newspaper underneath makes it easy to clean and change every few days. The water bottle should be wired to the cage three or four inches above the cage floor, and kept filled with fresh water at all times. You can buy processed food for them at pet or hardware stores and supplement this with fresh carrot strips and lettuce or leafy vegetables.

Your pet will stay healthy and friendly if you handle it gently and give it a daily run in your room.

Gerbils

Gerbils also make very successful pets and, chances are, if you don't keep some at home, you will study them in school. Like flying squirrels, they are extremely clean and healthy animals. They were originally imported from Egypt and other countries in Africa. A few of our states, such as California, have restrictions against selling or keeping gerbils, so you should check the regulations in your state before purchasing them.

Gerbils require a wire cage or terrarium, bedding and a water bottle similar to that suggested for hamsters and guinea pigs. The bedding should be changed and the cage cleaned every few days. They need an exercise wheel and also enjoy playing in and around small tin cans with the ends cut out. Gerbils need a varied diet and, like flying squirrels, stay frisky and happy on it. Try feeding them carrot strips, lettuce, sunflower seeds, fig newtons, apple slices and other foods you think they might like.

Be prepared for more than two gerbils if you buy a mated pair. They

The friendly gerbil is a favorite with many small children.

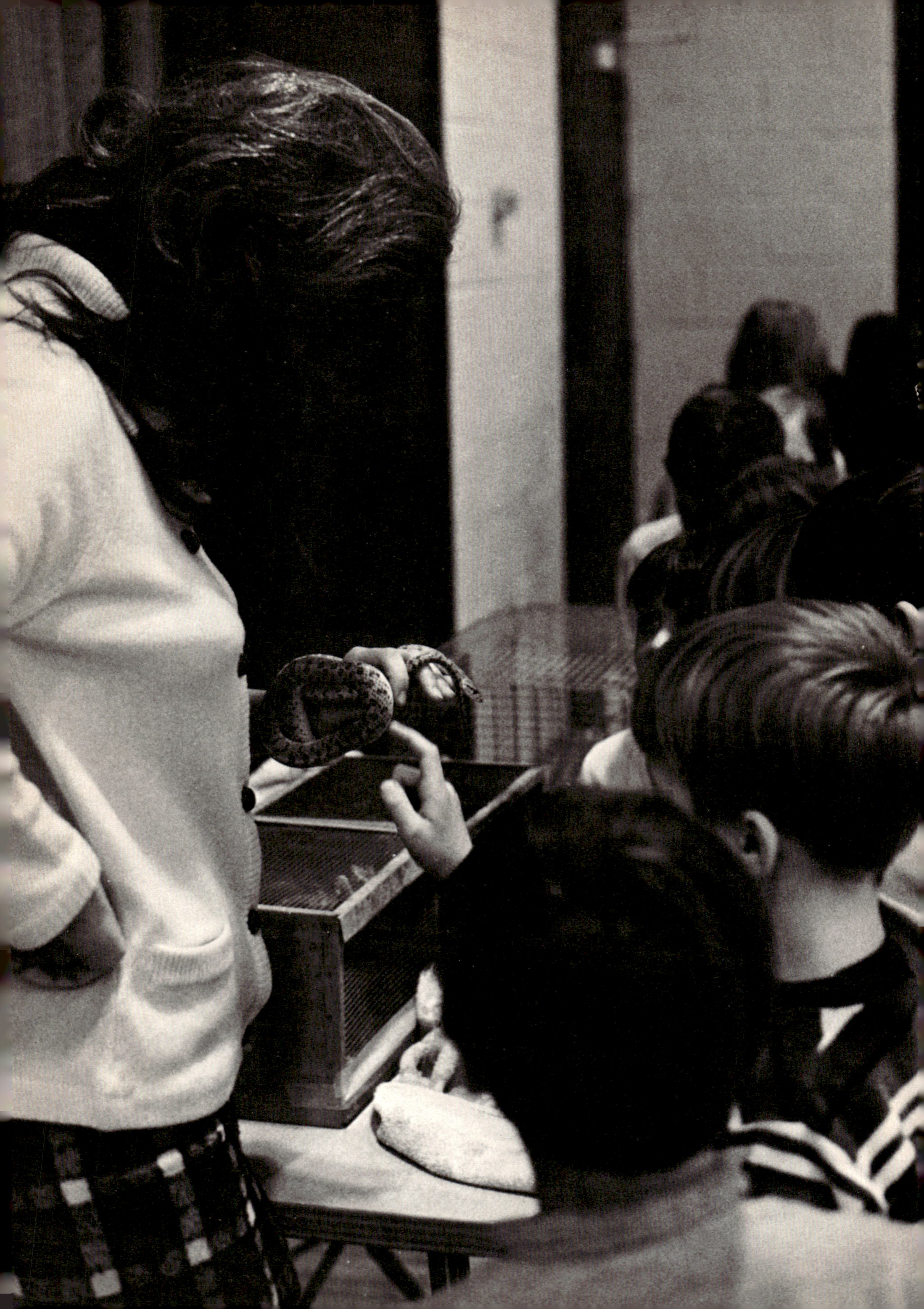

will soon present you with babies and, within a year, you may have as many as twenty to care for. If you keep them all, you will need several cages! Consider giving some to friends, to your school, or returning a few to the pet store in exchange for food to feed the ones you keep.

Whether you buy wild animals or collect them from fields, ponds and other areas; whether you keep them as pets or study projects; and whether you care for them over a long period of time or only a short one, keep in mind that animals are living things. They need food, care and kind treatment, just as you do. And because so many species are gradually dwindling in numbers in the face of man's invasion of their habitats, we all must do our share to protect and preserve them. While enjoying and studying the ways of your wild pets, be aware of how valuable each is to the balance of nature and the future of our environment.

One good way to learn about animals is by attending Nature Center study programs.

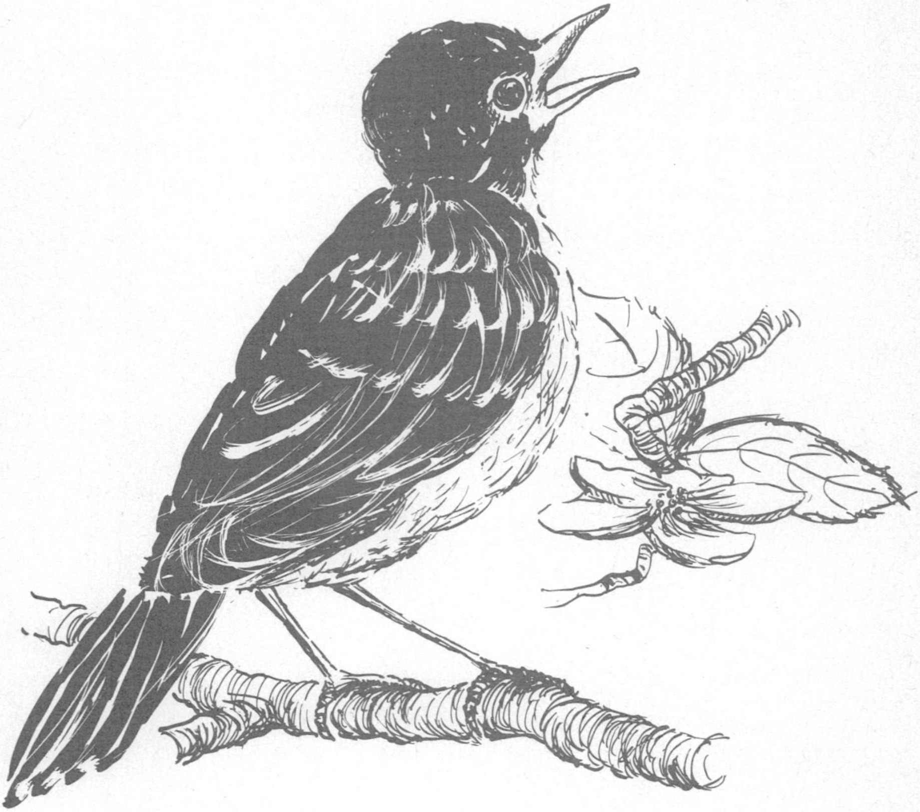

Additional Reading

INSECTS
Borror, D. J. and DeLong, D. M. *An Introduction to the Study of Insects*. New York: Rinehart, 1957.
Borror, D. J. and White, R. E. *A Field Guide to the Insects*. Boston: Houghton Mifflin, 1970.
Klots, A. E. and Klots, E. B. *Living Insects of the World*. New York: Doubleday, 1967.
Klots, A. E. *A Field Guide to the Butterflies*. Boston: Houghton Mifflin, 1964.
Lutz, F. E. *Field Book of Insects*. New York: Putnam, 1948.
Swain, R. B. *The Insect Guide*. New York: Doubleday, 1948.
Teale, E. W. *The Junior Book of Insects*. New York: E. P. Dutton & Co., 1966.
Zim, H. S. *Butterflies and Moths*. New York: Golden Press, 1964.
———. *Insects*. New York: Golden Press, 1956.

MARINE AQUARIA
Amos, W. H. *The Life of the Seashore*. New York: McGraw-Hill, 1966.
Buchsbaum, R. *Animals Without Backbones*. Chicago: University of Chicago Press, 1948.
Buchsbaum, R. and Milne, Lorus J. *The Lower Animals*. New York: Doubleday, 1961.
Hay, John. *The Sandy Shore*. Old Greenwich, Conn.: Chatham Press, 1968.
Kingsbury, J. M. *The Rocky Shore*. Old Greenwich, Conn.: Chatham Press, 1970.
Straughan, R. P. L. *The Salt-Water Aquarium in the Home*. New York: A. S. Barnes & Co., 1967.
White, L. B. *Life in the Shifting Dunes*. Boston: Museum of Science, 1960.
Zim, H. S. *Fishes*. New York: Golden Press, 1955.
———. *Seashores*. New York: Golden Press, 1955.

AMPHIBIANS
Porter, George. *The World of the Frog and the Toad*. New York: Lippincott, 1967.

REPTILES
Conant, R. *A Field Guide to Reptiles and Amphibians*. Boston: Houghton Mifflin, 1958.
Kauffeld, Carl. *Snakes: The Keeper and the Kept*. New York: Doubleday, 1969.
Schmidt, K. P. and Inger, R. F. *Living Reptiles of the World*. New York: Doubleday, 1957.
Villiard, Paul. *Reptiles as Pets*. New York: Doubleday, 1969.

MAMMALS
Brandt, L. *Raccoon Family Pets*. Wisconsin: All-Pets Books, Inc., 1954.
———. *Skunks as Pets*. Wisconsin: All-Pets Books, Inc., 1953.
Burt, W. H. and Grossenheider, R. P. *A Field Guide to the Mammals*. Boston: Houghton Mifflin, 1959.
Sanderson, I. T. *Living Mammals of the World*. New York: Doubleday, 1967.

WILD BIRDS
Gilliard, E. T. *Living Birds of the World.* New York: Doubleday, 1958.
Martin, A. G. *Hand-Taming Wild Birds at the Feeder.* Maine: Knowlton & McLeary Co.,

Peterson, R. T. *Field Guide to the Birds.* Boston: Houghton Mifflin, 1947.
Pettingill, O. S. *Enjoying Birds Around New York City.* Boston: Houghton Mifflin, 1966.
Robbins, C. S., Bruun, B. and Zim, H. S. *Birds of North America.* New York: Golden Press, 1966.
Terres, John K. *Songbirds in Your Garden.* New York: Thomas Y. Crowell Co., 1968.

GENERAL
Amos, W. H. *The Life of the Pond.* New York: McGraw-Hill, 1967.
Brown, Vinson. *How to Make a Miniature Zoo.* Boston: Little Brown & Co., 1957.
McCormick, Jack. *The Life of the Forest.* New York: McGraw-Hill, 1966.
Moore, C. B. *The Book of Wild Pets.* Boston: Charles T. Branford Co., 1954.
Niering, W. A. *The Life of the Marsh.* New York: McGraw-Hill, 1966.
Usinger, R. L. *The Life of Rivers and Streams.* New York: McGraw-Hill, 1967.

Index

Abdomen, 17
Alligator, 47
Amphibians, 17, 39-45, 47
Ants, 25-28
   army, 26
   carpenter, 26
   colonies, 26-27
   harvester, 26
   honey, 26
   leaf-cutting, 26
   observation house, 27
Aquarium, 13
   how to make, 13
   marine, 31-37
Arachnids, 18-19
Audubon Society of Connecticut, 72

Back swimmers, 23
Barnacles, 35-36
Bees, 17
Birds, 11, 17, 69-77
   care for wild birds, 73-77
   ducks, 77-79
   feeders, 70-71
   houses, 72-73
   observation checklist, 70
Butterflies, 23-24
   monarch, 24

Caddisfly, 21-23
   larvae, 21-23
Cages, how to build, 16
Caterpillars, 18, 23-24
Chipmunk, 11, 57
Chub, *see* killifish
Cocoons
   caterpillar, 18, 23-24
   praying mantis, 25
Cold-blooded, definition of, 39, 47
Collecting equipment, 16
Conservation, 7-9, 79-80
   rules, 9
Crabs, 33-35
   blue, 34

Calico, 34
fiddler, 34-35
green, 34
hermit, 33-34
horseshoe, 34
Jonah, 34
rock, 34
Crocodile, 47

Daddy longlegs, *see* harvestmen
Damselfly, 21
  nymph, 21
Dragonfly, 19-21
  nymph, 19-21

Exercise wheels, how to make, 59
Exotic species, 8, 79-80

Fish, 11, 17, 28, 32-33
  tropical, 79, 80-81
Fox, 11
Frogs, 11, 16, 20, 28, 39-45
  bullfrog, 39-40
  grass, 39-40
  green, 39-40
  spotted leopard, 39-40
  wood, 45
Fruit fly, 28-29

Gerbils, 16, 67, 79, 87
Guinea pig, 67, 79, 85

Habitat, definition of, 11
Hamster, 67, 79, 85
Harvestmen, 18-19
Head, 17

Insects, 16, 17-29
  Insectarium, 19
  Pet-food, 28-29
Invertebrates, definition of, 17

Killifish, 32

Larva, definition of, 18
Lizards, 28, 43, 47, 54-55
  anole, 54
  chameleon, *see* anole
  fence, 54-55
  gecko, 54
  horned toad, 54-55
  iguana, 54, 79
  skink, 54, 55

Mammals, 17, 28, 47, 57-67
Meal worms, 28-29
Mice, 57-59, 67, 79
  white-footed or deer, 58
  meadow mouse or vole, 58
Mites, 18-19
Minnow, *see* killifish
Moth, 23-24
Mussels, 37

Nature Centers, 8
  Junior Staff programs, 8
Newt, *see* salamander
Nymph, definition of, 18

Pipefish, 32-33
Plankton, 36
Polliwogs, *see* tadpoles
Porpoise, 57

Praying mantis, 24-25
Pupa, definition of, 18

Rabbits, 11, 16, 57, 61, 67, 79
Raccoons, 16, 57, 62-66, 67
Reptiles, 17, 47-55

Salamanders, 11, 16, 28, 39, 43-45
   mud puppy, 45
   red-spotted newt, 43-45
   spotted, 45
   two-lined, 43-45
Salentia, 41
Science museums, 8
Scorpions, 18-19
Sea anemone, 36-37
Seahorse, 33
Short-term pets, definition of, 8
Shrimp, 35
Skunk, 57, 66-67
Snails, 33, 37
   periwinkle, 33, 37
   moon snail, 33, 37
   mud snail, 37
   whelk, 33, 37
Snakes, 16, 28, 47, 49, 51-54
   black, 51
   garter, 47, 51, 53
   glass, 54
   water, 47
   musk, 51
   painted, 50-51
   snapping, 51
   stinkpot, *see* musk turtle
   sun, *see* painted turtle
   wood, 50
Spiders, 18-19
Spinneret, 24
Starfish, 37
Squirrel, 11, 16, 57, 59-61, 67
   flying, 67, 79, 84-85

Tadpoles, 39-45
Terrarium, 11-13, 16
Thorax, 17
Ticks, 18-19
Toads, 28, 39, 41-42, 45
Turtles, 16, 28, 47, 49-51
   box, 49-50

Vertebrates, definition of, 17

Walking stick, 25
Wasps, 17
Whales, 57

Zoologist, 7